MYSTICISM AND DEMOCRACY IN THE ENGLISH COMMONWEALTH

Mysticism and Democracy in the English Commonwealth

Being the William Belden Noble Lectures delivered in Harvard University, 1930–1931

BY

RUFUS M. JONES

1 9 6 5

OCTAGON BOOKS, INC.

NEW YORK

Reprinted 1965
by special arrangement with Harvard University Press

OCTAGON BOOKS, INC.
175 FIFTH AVENUE
NEW YORK, N. Y. 10010

LIBRARY OF CONGRESS CATALOG CARD NUMBER: 65-16774

Printed in U.S.A. by
NOBLE OFFSET PRINTERS, INC.
NEW YORK 3, N. Y.

TO MY WIFE

ELIZABETH BARTRAM JONES
whose coöperative help in the work of research
involved in these chapters was invaluable,
I dedicate this book with affection-
ate appreciation

THE
WILLIAM BELDEN NOBLE
LECTURES

THIS LECTURESHIP WAS CONSTITUTED A PER-
PETUAL FOUNDATION IN HARVARD UNIVERSITY IN
1898, AS A MEMORIAL TO THE LATE WILLIAM BEL-
DEN NOBLE OF WASHINGTON, D.C. (HARVARD,
1885). THE DEED OF GIFT PROVIDES THAT THE
LECTURES SHALL BE NOT LESS THAN SIX IN NUM-
BER, THAT THEY SHALL BE DELIVERED ANNUALLY,
AND, IF CONVENIENT, IN THE PHILLIPS BROOKS
HOUSE, DURING THE SEASON OF ADVENT. EACH
LECTURER SHALL HAVE AMPLE NOTICE OF HIS
APPOINTMENT, AND THE PUBLICATION OF EACH
COURSE OF LECTURES IS REQUIRED. THE PURPOSE
OF THE LECTURESHIP WILL BE FURTHER SEEN IN
THE FOLLOWING CITATION FROM THE DEED OF
GIFT BY WHICH IT WAS ESTABLISHED:

THE WILLIAM BELDEN NOBLE LECTURES

"The object of the founder of the Lectures is to continue the mission of William Belden Noble, whose supreme desire it was to extend the influence of Jesus as the way, the truth, and the life; to make known the meaning of the words of Jesus, 'I am come that they might have life, and that they might have it more abundantly.' In accordance with the large interpretation of the Influence of Jesus by the late Phillips Brooks, with whose religious teaching he in whose memory the Lectures are established and also the founder of the Lectures were in deep sympathy, it is intended that the scope of the Lectures shall be as wide as the highest interests of humanity. With this end in view, — the perfection of the spiritual man and the consecration by the spirit of Jesus of every department of human character, thought, and activity, — the Lectures may include philosophy, literature, art, poetry, the natural sciences, political economy, sociology, ethics, history, both civil and ecclesiastical, as well as theology and the more direct interests of the religious life. Beyond a sympathy with the purpose of the Lectures, as thus defined, no restriction is placed upon the lecturer."

INTRODUCTION

MASSON's *Life of Milton*, Carlyle's *Life and Letters of Oliver Cromwell* and Barclay's *Inner Life of the Religious Societies of the Commonwealth* made every reader of those books aware that this Commonwealth period of great events and significant personalities was also a time of profound religious ferment. In Germany Weingarten, Troeltsch, and Sippell, to mention only three scholars, took up, with characteristic German thoroughness, the study of this religious ferment to discover its connection with the English Reformation and its bearing upon later religious developments in England. When I was preparing my volume on *The Spiritual Reformers of the Sixteenth and Seventeenth Centuries* (London, 1914), I became convinced that there were many movements and currents of thought in that period still to be explored and mapped out. The practical tasks and problems of the war and its aftermath left no time nor freedom for the remote issues of bygone centuries. But when a breathing space came in the autumn of 1929 I seized upon it for a period of research in the British Museum, hoping especially to trace more carefully than had yet been done the origin and development of the English "Seekers."

As I pursued my studies I soon became impressed with the close connection between the re-

ligious movements of this stormy period and the
political issues which were then being settled. It
seemed clearly demonstrable that the new stage in
the development of English democracy, which is
marked by the Commonwealth period, was inti-
mately tied into these religious movements with
which I was engaged. I have therefore endeavored
to show what an important epoch that great period
was for the maturing of the religious life of England, and equally so for its bold experiments in
popular self-government, first tried in the democratic religious sects and then carried out in the
wider area of the State.

We are passing through an era of disillusionment
over the high hopes and expectations which once
centred in the democratic experiment. It broke in
on men's minds with revolutionary fervor, and with
it came the glowing dream that at last the solution
was to be found for all political ills and for age-old
injustices. Wars were fought in the enthusiastic
hope that the world would be made safe through
democracy and for democracy. There has come a
sudden depression and slump of faith in democracy,
and the word does not now carry quite its old-time
magic.

The slump is almost certainly a temporary one.
There are weaknesses inherent in any human form
of government, and they are only too evident in the
democratic form, but it can safely be predicted
that men will never again be satisfied with any
type of government in which they do not share.

But democracy cannot succeed without sound educational preparation for it. Nor will it ever be a true success without a deep moral and religious background in the lives of the people who compose the democratic government. The upward reach of man's life for spiritual guidance is as important as is the outward reach of fellowship from man to man. Democracy will slowly and surely come back to its own, chastened by wisdom and suffering.

It may be worth while in the interim to turn back to see how close was the religious bond in the great birth period of democracy, when a noble spiritual mysticism was one and inseparable with high-minded democracy.

CONTENTS

MYSTICISM AND DEMOCRACY

I

A GREAT AWAKENING

THE hour has struck, I think, for a great spiritual awakening in our modern world. We are running on low gear, or, as the pre-automobile age would have said, we are going "at a jog-trot" gait. We have encompassed the old mountains around and around long enough. We need to hear a voice that carries authority, saying to us, "Go forward and take possession of new land." But spiritual advances and great awakenings do not come at command, nor can they be staged by some ingenious contrivance. There is always a mystery attaching to the movings of the Spirit. There is something about the coming and the going of epochs which change the line of march or shift the levels of life, that escapes our most subtle analysis.

The reason why we cannot plan such movements and inaugurate them by skilful campaign methods is that there is something vastly more involved than a set of ideas, or than a body of well rationalized thought which can be summed up and interpreted after the movement has run its course and is over. While it is on and is inwardly alive it stirs the profoundest emotions of men's being. It creates great systems of interest and of sentiment. It sets regions boiling and effervescing far below the thought-level. Immense energies are liberated which ordinarily would not attach to the words and ideas that become the current coin of the period. Lives become charged and energized. I shall deal here with such an epoch as that.

The era of the English Commonwealth, taken broadly to cover the years from the beginning of the Long Parliament in 1640 to the restoration of the Stuarts in 1660, is beyond question one of the most momentous and dynamic periods in the entire range of English history. If we take into reckoning not only this short twenty-year span but also the period of a generation before it, when the religious and political processes were emerging that made the Commonwealth Era possible, we shall perhaps find ourselves dealing with the most creative single epoch in the modern life of England. It was, too, a birth-period for colonial life in America. The congregational type of religious organization was born in that period, and out of that experiment the immense discovery was made that the democratic principle and method of handling affairs could be expanded and extended from a self-governing Church to a self-governing State. That expansion is an important part of my story. There was yeast enough present in that new social order to leaven the three centuries that have followed since.

Great awakenings, like that which characterize the Commonwealth Era, always present, as I have said, an element of surprise and mystery. They are similar in some respects to biological "mutations."

They are unique and novel. They are unpre-
dictable. They involve the break up of age-long
established forms and models that have gone on in
unvarying and repeatable fashion, and the sudden
emergence of some new form or type that never
was before. I have called these awakenings mysterious, and so they are. But they are apparently
not miraculous. It is possible to trace many of the
forces and influences that shape the new currents of
life and thought in such an epoch. So many lines
of potentiality and tendency can be discovered in
the years before the awakening burst forth that
one is at first inclined to assert that nothing novel
happened and that the so-called mutation event
was only the pre-determined result of existent,
though latent, driving forces. But the fact remains
that when all the curves of tendency that were
there before have been minutely studied and all the
operating forces have been marshaled and plotted
out, there is no way to establish an equation between what was there before and the new thing
that is there now. There has come a sudden disintegration of the repeatable forms of life and
thought, and with that disintegration the emergence of new insights, novel adventures, and unique
experiments.

Sometimes, of course, such mutation awakenings have proved to be futile, just as "sports" in
the biological order often prove to be abortive.
They do not inaugurate anything significant.
They do not shift the line of march. They intro-

duce no new power of advance. It is, however, possible to count up a pretty long list of epochs of awakening when something has emerged that has had ever after to be reckoned with in the life of the race and in the progress of the world. Such awakenings set free creative forces. They put into operation constructive energies that mark an absolute difference between the earlier date and the later one. Such times of awakening are watershed epochs in the life of the race. Like great mountain divides, from that point onward they turn all currents in a new direction.

It is my purpose in these studies to show what an outburst of fresh insight and what an increase of vitality characterized this epoch of the Commonwealth. There was much that was chaotic, fantastic and erratic. It was not a well-ordered onward ground-swell. There were backwashes and side-swirls in the movement. The new freedom turned many heads. The surge and drive of the times swept along fanatics and addle-brained persons as well as geniuses and creative leaders. The ferment, as is true with all ferments, ministered to the production of intoxicants as well as to the production of foods. Consequently we shall need to take account in this story of losses as well as of gains. In fact what I am calling a great awakening has seemed to some historians a period of perversity and regression. Contemporary writers were loud in their laments over the degeneracy of the times. What seems to me to have been the leaven of a new spiritual epoch seemed to them at the time the dregs and corruption of a good world gone wrong — "the very dregs and spawn of old accustomed heresies which had been already condemned, dead, buried and rotten in their graves long ago," as the guardians of the old time religion expressed it.

The most obvious feature of this period of awakening was the intensity of *faith* that characterized it. There was a strange variety of opinions and interpretations, but all the movements had one point in common. They all revealed a high degree of spiritual *caloric*. There was an unmistakable driving power operating in them. The leaders and prophets knew that they had discovered something that was real and something that was important. They were oracles of the glowing positive. In fact the first half of the seventeenth century in England witnessed a genuine revival of that same type of white-hot faith that worked so mightily at the heart of the Reformation on the Continent a century earlier. The differences in thought and outlook were unmistakable, but the quality of faith was strikingly similar.

The English Reformation in the sixteenth century lacked precisely that inner depth and intensity of spiritual motive which were so great a feature of Luther's power. It was sicklied o'er with a pale cast of political aim and purpose. It had no guiding prophet. It was weak in vision. There was no one who could authoritatively de-

clare, "Thus saith the Lord." No one had that
gift of genius that could fuse the whole nation with
a clear sense of direction and raise it to a new spiritual level. Names were changed, practices were
altered, the status of ownership and dominion was
shifted, but there was no burst of hot lava from
within the souls of men that made everything new.
Henry VIII, Edward VI, Queen Mary and Queen
Elizabeth guided or repressed the movement as
their policy directed, but the Tudors were not
prophets: they were sovereigns. And whatever
else James I may have been, he was neither a prophet nor the son of a prophet! Nor, we may add,
was he the father of one!

Slowly, however, through the ripening of forces
that were latent in the Lollard movement, through
the kindling work of the Continental leaders and
prophets and the quickening power of their books,
a new life and an inward faith began to take shape
in the hearts and minds of English men and women.
As usual the attempts at repression or extermina-
tion only fanned the flame of faith to a more glowing heat. For an entire century the cumulative
processes went forward. The ferment was working
all the time, but its immense transforming power
was hardly suspected until the internal explosive
force suddenly burst the old containers in the up-
heaval of the Commonwealth Era.

It is an interesting question what it is that
makes faith, which often seems dead and undyna-
mic, become so alive and powerful at certain epochs

of history. Men drone along with religious words and phrases. They shuffle back and forth their stock of ideas and doctrines. Then suddenly a new breath blows across the world, an intense faith is born, and the same words and phrases, and almost the same ideas and doctrines, become quick and vital. The new faith makes lethargy henceforth impossible. It produces a revaluation of all values. It undermines old systems and customs and over-throws the most solidly established dynasties, both of empire and of thought. What is the strange secret of it? Where does the dynamic come from?

The psychology of the situation is fairly plain, though as always happens with psychology it can-not probe to the heart of this human mystery. Somebody succeeds in formulating an idea about this life of ours with such depth and reality that it dominates the field of attention. It takes the focus point of one's inner being, the way a bright object draws the fovea of the retina away from everything else to that. It unifies what was before a divided self. Around this focal point within a unique in-tegration takes place. The dissipated and scattered forces of the mind that usually are more or less at war within the person are now fused together into a single ground-swell movement. Instead of sun-dered parts functioning in turn there is one un-divided whole within. Contra-suggestions make no impression now. Inhibitions are not heard. Marginal processes and the fringy haloes that ordinarily tend to draw us away from our focal ideas now all pull in the same direction. It becomes well-nigh impossible to think the opposite of the idea that fills the whole centre of the internal stage.

Ideas that possess that focalizing power, that integrating quality, naturally succeed in getting the entire self of the person behind them. It is absurd to say that they have a high emotional quality and that they possess a strong driving power toward action, since all ideas have some emotional quality and all ideas are in some degree propulsive. The trouble is that in our ordinary lives the checking and restraining tendencies in us neutralize or inhibit the emotional and propulsive character of our thoughts. One part in us says "yes" but another part says "no." We "propose," but our habits and inhibitions "dispose." Like Penelope we unweave what we weave. We carry opposing teams within ourselves, and our souls are arenas for contests of victory and defeat instead of being the scene of one single dominating actor that does what is done.

This inward unification not only masses all the combined forces of our *conscious* ideas and purposes, but what is, perhaps, even more important, it opens, in a way that is still mysterious, hidden doors to vast reservoirs of energies in us that lie below the threshold of consciousness. We say, in casual fashion, of a person who "wakes up" that he has "found himself" — that he has "come to himself." When one does *that* he does more than merely find any self that ever was before: he gets all of himself that he has ever taken any account of, together with an extraordinary increment of range and power. Faith, at its best, is the discovery of a truth or an idea that has that marvelous unifying or integrating power and that at the same time releases the deep-lying energies that are needed for the complete liberation of one's whole self.

This emergence of dynamic faith is a characteristic feature of all great awakenings. Whether it be Gautama Buddha that inaugurates the awakening or Francis of Assisi, the expansive quality of faith that marks it will be the one common feature in the midst of differences of race and epoch, of intellectual content and cultural background. So, too, in the period which I am studying, the religious awakening of the seventeenth century had a great variety of different forms and manifestations. It differentiated into numerous specific lines of movement, with notably different mental content in each and with a varying body of aims and ideas. Each specific movement had its own coherent currents of thought and its peculiar principles of organization, its party cries and its slogans, but they were all alike in one respect: they dynamized their adherents with a new unifying energy of faith.

The differentiated movements of our period fall quite naturally into four characteristic religious types, each one of which links with a definite parent stream of historical influence. The first type, and the one with which I shall deal most extensively in these lectures, is the one that is best called mystical. It, in turn, took on a great variety of forms and expressions which with difficulty reduce to a single type. The "Cambridge Platonists" and the "Familists" for instance, are as unlike as two groups of persons can well be, and yet they were both alike in one central claim which they made, that they had direct and first-hand experience of God. There have been few periods in any country, and no others in England, that have been so intensely and profoundly mystical as was this first half of the seventeenth century. It was a highly fertile flowering time of the mystical life.

The English people are not as a rule mystically inclined. There were, to be sure, in the fourteenth century, a few highly gifted English men and women who were contemplative geniuses of a high order and who at the same time were able to interpret their rich experience of God in noble literary style. The mystical books of that period show in a profound degree the influence of the great Roman Catholic mystics of the Continent and, with the peculiar variations due to race and intellectual climate, they carry on the Neo-Platonic tradition set by the famous mystic of the early sixth century whom we call by his pseudonym, "Dionysius the Areopagite." This new outburst of English mysticism in the seventeenth century, of which I am speaking, was of a very different type. It did not follow the classical Catholic models. It was not "a flight of the alone to the Alone." Its goal was not ecstacy. It was not in any marked degree characterized by a pattern scale of ascents — a mystic Jacob's Ladder.

Its method was not in any proper sense a *via negativa* path to God. God was not thought of by these mystics as an absolute Other — as a Great Unknown and Unknowable, an infinite Beyond. For this reason Roman Catholic authorities would not admit that the word mysticism is rightly applied to this seventeenth-century occurrence of intense experience of God. These authorities, and with them some Protestant scholars of the subject, confine the word mysticism sharply to that single negative type of experience. To be a mystic in their sense of the word is to be raised by a special act of divine Grace into contact or union with God in a way that transcends all the normal capacities of human reason, with the result that the limits of human nature are overpassed and the experient attains an unutterable state — unutterable precisely because the state that is reached is beyond the range of human powers, and has to do with a realm of realities for which there are no terms of thought and for which no language has been coined. It is a *super-mind* attainment.

I have always used the word mysticism with a much wider meaning, and shall continue to do so. The essential feature of a mystical experience as I view it is not the negative path of approach nor the special scale of ladder-steps upward, nor the empty-handed, or *nirvana*, state in which the experience culminates. Its essential aspect is rather the *conviction of certainty* that the person's own soul has found its goal of reality in God. God is no longer a

Being to argue about, to prove by logic, or to be merely read of in a Book from a remote past; He is here and now, can be met by the way and can become as real to the awakened soul as Gibraltar is to the mariner who sails through the Straits.

Isaac Penington, a Seeker and later "a happy Finder," in an experience that came to him in 1658, declared with rapturous words: "This is He, this is He. There is no other: This is He whom I have waited for and sought after from my childhood. . . . I have met with my God; I have met with my Saviour. I have felt the healings drop upon my soul from under His wings." [1] That is quite unlike a passage from Meister Eckhart or from Lady Julian or any other fourteenth-century mystic, but it presents in vivid and intense language a personal consciousness of fellowship and relationship between man and God, a consciousness that brought with it an immense transformation of life. Penington is only one of a multitude of Seekers and saints in this seventeenth-century period who found themselves flooded with light and life and power that seemed to them to be from the Source of light and life and power, and in the sense of healing and joy that came to them they were convinced that they were walking in the newness of life with God. Their hearts burned as they walked with Him. They were affirmation mystics rather than of the negative type, but I see no reason for denying such

[1] *Works*, I, 37–38.

an extension of meaning to the word as this involves. Penington says with a touch of beauty, "The soul begotten by the Divine Breath depends on it for continual breathing. Nothing hath so much of God and yet nothing is so little able to live without Him." I shall not stop now to trace the historical roots of this type of life and thought, but we may take for granted that it had historical roots and we shall endeavor to find them later on.

There was in evidence in the second place a very strong humanistic strain of thought. It is not easy to separate the mystical strand from the humanistic because they appear united in many persons of the period and in a number of movements of the time. In some the mystical note is dominant, and in others the humanistic is central. Sometimes they are happily blended and sometimes, again, only one or the other of the two aspects is noticeable. It is the fruit of the noble humanism of Erasmus, Colet, Sir Thomas More, Edmund Spenser, Sir Philip Sidney and of the spiritual reformers, of whom there will be much to say later. The great parent of this movement is of course Plato, together with his greatest mystical-minded disciple, Plotinus. It was characterized by an immense faith in the fundamental nature of reason, thought of as a divine capacity of the human soul. There is, they all assume, something majestic, even Godlike, in the inmost structure of man's being. Even the catastrophe of the Fall, which Plato as well as "Moses" described, did not carry its dev-

astating ruin into this citadel of the soul. When
everything else was "lost" this God-given Reason,
this participation of man in the eternal *nous*, remained unlost and inalienable. That humanistic
principle of optimism was an obvious basis for a
mystical view of life, and many of the persons
whom we shall meet in these lectures took their
stand as will appear on that high ground.

There was in the third place a strong wave of
pantheistical sentiment abroad, both on the Continent and in England. Its parentage is not so
easily traced as is that of the other prevailing
types of thought, but it, too, had its source and
background. The widespread pantheistic-mystical
sects of the fourteenth century were never exter-
minated; they were rather driven down out of sight
and became a submerged stream of influence.
There were pretty plain up-wellings of this stream
during the Reformation period in Europe in the
sixteenth century and, like most of the religious
currents that had their birth on the Continent in
this time of turmoil, it revived in England a century later. It was, furthermore, perfectly easy and
natural to find pantheism in the Platonism that
was current in England from the time of the
Renaissance onward. Humanistic Platonism was
saturated with a Neo-Platonic tinge, and it took
no effort to push this over into pantheism. Besides
that, the Europe of the sixteenth century had become literally fascinated with the pantheism of the
Jewish Cabbalah, and there are unmistakable

traces of its influence on the thought of seventeenth-century England. This pantheism from
these different sources had many close links both
with the humanism and with the mysticism that
will meet us as we proceed.

There was a fourth type of religious movement
which was by far the most extensive and the most
impressive feature of the age, though it will receive
very little treatment in these pages. I mean, of
course, the central Puritan movement. It is cus-
tomary in the present age to see the Puritans
through the reverse end of the glass, to belittle
them and to belabor them. Their seriousness of-
fends our generation, their sternness irritates, their
infallibilities seem absurd, their precise legalism
revolts us. They are pictured as the victims of re-
pressions and complexes. It is assumed that they
were hypocritical, or, if not, then self-deceived
fanatics, who made God's world as difficult a place
to live in as possible. They are supposed to have
hated the beautiful and the lovely features of life
and to have been a race of kill-joy pilgrims, concerned only with their own election to a post-
mortem paradise.

Such pictures are artificial, and most of the off-
hand accounts that flourish today are unhistorical
and imaginary. The real Puritan of history who
walked the earth three hundred years ago was built
on great architectural lines and was, and still remains, an awe-inspiring figure. Religion for him
did not mean a dash of rose-water perfume sprayed

on for a rare occasion or for a brief sacramental moment. It was the whole business of life. It was just because God was so tremendously real, and the issues and destiny of life were of such eternal significance, that temporal joys and sorrows were foreshortened for him and shrank to slight importance. I do not share the view that a vision of eternal destiny makes temporal matters unimportant, but I can at least appreciate the way that estimate affected and exalted the seventeenth-century Puritan. I wish he had found his way of life revealed in the spirit of the New Testament, rather than in the legal covenant of the Hebrew Commonwealth, but I cannot blame him for concluding with the wisest scholars of his age that every word of the Old Testament was a Word of God. What I do admire in him is the resolute will of the man to take that Word of God seriously and to set about the task of building a new commonwealth according to the pattern which he found revealed in the Mount. The Calvinistic system and plan of life which formed the backbone of the seventeenth-century Puritan was an imperial structure of thought that could compete in dignity, in grandeur and in august authority with the Roman Catholic system itself, to a degree that no other reformation movement achieved. The reformed city-state in Geneva, the United Netherlands, the unconquerable Huguenots of France, the new Scotland of John Knox, the English Commonwealth of the seventeenth century and the New

England that the Puritan exiles built leave no
question of the robustness and the virility of the
movement. There was a quality of structural steel
about it. It may be spent now, and it may have
collapsed like the one-horse shay, but it was very
much alive once, and its effect on the development
of modern history is and will always remain a fact
of major importance.

So far as Puritanism was a system of religious
thought and interpretation, it was essentially
forensic rather than mystical. The Puritan arrived
at his view of God, of the universe and of life, not
through some transforming personal experience
that opened a window for his soul into another
realm of reality, but rather by a logical and argumentative interpretation of great texts of Scripture, which for him were the literal words of God,
once for all supernaturally revealed to man. He
did not look inward for his basic truths: he turned
to his sacred Book, and took it as settled beyond
controversy that God's covenant as expressed in
that Book was the pattern for the saints of all
time.

That the Scriptures were the word of God was
not a matter of debate for him: it was to his mind
an axiom of his religion. The opposite of it was
unthinkable. Without this sure foundation as a
basis the whole structure of his faith and thought,
the entire conception of creation and salvation,
would have fallen like Jericho at the sound of the
rams' horns. His conclusions, however they may

seem to us to be forensic and argumentative rather than inherently self-evident, were for him of the nature of absolute truth. The mystic who rested his faith on his own experience did not have a more invincible conviction than did the Puritan with his truths buttressed upon the Word of God which could not lie. Few believers have ever lived who have had a greater sense of infallibility. It no longer seems to most of us a possible way of approach, but it gave two generations of men a vigorous grip on pen and sword and it was a world-building faith.

The Puritan had no confidence, such as the humanist quite naturally had, in man's native capacity of reason. He considered that the ruin of the Fall ran through the whole range of the universe, and left its taint and blight on all that belonged to human nature. Man himself was a mass of corruption, and could do nothing in his own power to rehabilitate himself. The Puritan had two ugly words with which he disposed of all claims to innate human capacity for spiritual achievement. He called it forthwith a brand of "Pelagianism," revived through the instigation of the same old over-busy Devil that originated it, or it was blasted with scorn as "Arminianism," a more recent concoction of evil leaven brought from the kitchen of the Dutch heretic, Arminius, whose very name was a hissing and an opprobrium.

Edwards, in his dragnet of all heresies which he called *The Gangraena, or a Catalogue and Discovery of*

Errours, Heresies and Blasphemies, counted up in the
middle of the seventeenth century no less than one
hundred and ninety-nine sects and schisms that
broke out to disturb the peace of the infallible-
minded Puritans in their hour of victory. The
Children of Israel reached their Promised Land
only to find that the Hittites and Hivites and
Canaanites and Perizzites and Girgashites and
Amorites and Jebusites were there waiting to contend for every inch of ground with the chosen of
the Lord. So it was again in the day of Puritan
success: heresies swarmed like locusts threatening
to devour every green herb of the precious truth.
Marsden in his *Later Puritans* says: "Opinions
monstrous and prodigious started up every day
and were broached with impunity in public and
private, and multitudes were led astray. The number of new sects, religious and political, with which
England swarmed appears almost incredible. The
sober Puritans were confounded. The state of
England reminded them of the fabulous description
of the sands of Libya, where scorching suns produce new monsters every year." [1]

Old Ephraim Pagitt concluded that the English
people of his time must belong to the "Tribe of
Gad," a mad race of runners-about and gadders
and seducers. He appealed to the Mayor of London in 1645 to save his city from "infection."
"The plague," he said, "is of all diseases most in-
fectious: I have lived among you almost a jubile,

[1] Marsden's *Later Puritans* (London, second edition), p. 224.

and have seen your great care and provision to keep the city from infection. The plague of heresy is greater, and you are now in more danger than when you buried five thousand a week. You have power to keep these heretics and sectaries from conventickling and sholing together to infect one another." [1]

It would appear that one of the main tasks of ancient mayors was to prevent the "bootlegging" of that peculiar type of spirit which we call religious ideas. And it would furthermore appear to have been hardly less easy to prevent that kind of bootlegging than it is to prevent the kind that worries our civic officers today.

The most famous of all the contemporary accounts of this extraordinary outbreak of the bootlegging of religious ideas, which so disturbed the peace of the guardians of the truth is the one given by Milton in the *Areopagitica* in 1644: "I see a noble and puissant nation rousing herself like a strong man after a sleep and shaking her invincible locks. Methinks I see her, as an eagle mewing her mighty youth and kindling her undazzled eyes at the full mid-day beam, purging and unsealing her long abused sight at the fountain itself of heavenly radiance, while the whole noise of timorous and flocking birds, with those also that love the twilight, flutter about amazed at what she means and in their envious gabble would prognosticate a year of sects and schisms."

[1] Pagitt's *Heresiography* (London, 1645), Dedication.

Milton, however, notwithstanding his unique power to describe the notorious activities of these bootleggers of new religions, was himself an impenitent "wet." His book was written not to condemn nor to urge the suppression of this free activity of thought but to plead for the right of human minds to seek for themselves, to find for themselves and to express in their own way what seemed to them to be the truth. It is one of the noblest pieces of prose in our language, and one of the loftiest declarations of the liberty of human thought in any language.

It remains only for me to say a few words in this first lecture about the fundamental influence that lies back of this awakening, and that was the main spur and spring that produced the epoch. There were many secondary influences, as I have intimated, but the primary one was plainly enough that marvelous book, the English Bible. Luther's German Bible was a work of genius, and it acted like magic on the minds of its readers, but an even greater masterpiece of genius was the English Bible of 1611. There are few literary creations in the whole range of human writings that can compare with it in its quality of beauty and harmony, and none, I think, that match the spiritual power of it. It must be taken into account at every point in every one of the religious movements of the period with which we are concerned. It formed the very warp and woof of the thought of every leader, and the followers were almost equally at home in it.

It was literally the possession of the mind of every person who counted for anything.

Already, before the King James translators had done their perfect work, William Tyndale had set the model for it and had given the readers of the Bible in Elizabeth's reign a translation of extraordinary merit. In fact more than half of the King James version was taken over with little alteration from the work of that noble martyr, who sat through cold winter nights, shivering in his Belgian dungeon before the door opened for him to go out to the fire that burned him. During the entire formative period before the Commonwealth, and in the flowering epoch of it, the English Bible was the constant inspiration that made this period such a rich fruition time in the Anglo-Saxon world.

Without much doubt, issues of eternal destiny were the major factors in the formation of these intensified groups. They worked on the minds of men like immense driving energies. Some modern historians have labored to show that economic interests were the controlling forces. It is a fact beyond question that economic factors have a subtle way of creeping on the stage and playing their rôle without being consciously known or recognized. And they were there in the seventeenth century, either behind the scenes or full in the picture, but it was not the thought of houses or lands, or estates or crops, that gave the touch of white heat to the souls of these men. They were in dead earnest about unseen and eternal realities. And it may be

taken as settled that we have lost the clue to an
understanding of them when we have left out the
religious aspects of their lives. "Only think," said
Vinet of his own country, "so much liberty and no
beliefs!" That is quite characteristic of easy-going
periods of civilization but not of great awakenings.

I have taken as the main subject of these studies
"Mysticism and Democracy." I am undertaking
to show that the intense religious life of the period,
together with the creation of the self-governing
type of church, had a powerful influence in bringing
democracy to birth in the State. In a certain sense
a true and genuine democracy is inherently and in-
trinsically mystical in character. A democracy in
which the individuals remain atomic units, self-
centred and stubbornly sundered one from the
other, merely pooling their judgments, in the form
of votes, to secure ends that could be attained in no
other way, would of course have nothing mystical
about it. But a democracy in which the individuals
are fused into a living organic group so that each
individual finds his wisdom and insight heightened
through his group life and team work for common
ends is at heart a mystical order. There is something more in each individual than there would be
if he were operating alone in isolation. He becomes
in a real sense *over-individual*, and transcends himself through the life of others. The group somehow
contributes a plus quality to each organic member
of it. This mystical group influence appeared in
primitive times in the totem-groups where through

clan sympathy and solidarity the individuals of the
tribe discovered the gleam of an immortal hope and
the possibility of some kind of survival after death.
It appeared again in the creation of mythology
among imaginative races. The early myths and
explanations were the creative work of corporate
groups rather than the achievements of isolated
individuals, and each participant had the imaginative quality of his life heightened by what they
all did together as a group.

This principle is most obvious in the group experiences of the early apostolic churches. The
groups at Pentecost, in the gatherings for com-
munal meals together and in the high-tide fellowships for worship — "in one Spirit baptized into
one body" — rolled up a cumulative wisdom
which every one shared. The memory of the past,
the expectancy as to the future and the religious
emotion of the present, were no doubt important
factors, but wherever men are fused together in
common fellowship for common ends the individual
is over-passed and the whole is greater than the
sum of the parts. This situation was profoundly
true in the religious democracies which came to
birth in England in the seventeenth century, even
in the least mystical of them. They felt themselves
to be "blessed communities" in the sense that each
one was ennobled in and through his fellowship
with kindred minds, and this same spirit went
over to some degree into the larger democracies
which sprang out of the religious ones.

We have grown so vast in these modern times, so complex, so heterogeneous, that it is of all things difficult to preserve the inward sympathy and solidarity of the group life which make a democracy a mystical reality. Is it, however, a forlorn hope? Are we foredoomed to have the vision of the *Urbs Sion Mystica* fade out into the common day of party politics and machine rule, or can we come back to the task of rebuilding our nation of the people, for the people, by the people, as our noblest prophets have always seen that it ought to be? Perhaps this excursion into the history of a past epoch may quicken our hope.

II

BUILDING A SELF–GOVERNING CHURCH

WHEN the reformers of the sixteenth century set themselves to the task of reconstructing and re-organizing the Church, after their break with the ancient form and order of the historic Church, they naturally turned to the New Testament for guidance. They soon discovered that the guidance was not so precise and specific as they might have expected it to be. New Testament scholars are pretty well united now in the conclusion that during the first century there was no one sacred and essential type of church organization in operation. Great personalities, with unique gifts of ministry and leadership, played a much more significant part in the apostolic age than did any pattern system of organization. As we should expect would be the case, many experiments in method and system were made, in each instance adapted to the racial traits, the historic customs, and the long established habits of the particular region where a visiting prophet or apostle or evangelist gathered out a lit-tle *ecclesia*, which stood forth like a tiny island in a vast sea of pagan dwellers. These creative visitors carried with them no rigid architectural model of a church. They builded as well as they could out of the material at hand — sometimes "gold, silver, precious stones"; sometimes "hay, wood, and stubble" — and they allowed the new *ecclesia* of the region to take the line of development that best fitted the needs of the given people and the mental habits and background of the builder. The Church in Jerusalem was in almost every respect unlike the Church in Corinth.

The result is that the New Testament shows no settled and unalterable preference for one definite typical church. As one star differeth from another star in glory, so, too, one church in the great creative epoch differed from another church in its form and its order. It is no doubt quite easy for a modern churchman, who assumes that there can be no true Church unless its form can be derived from apostolic authority, to read his mental picture of the Church back into the New Testament and to find the model of it prescribed in the sacred writ. Scholars, however, who are historically trained and who read the record with unprejudiced minds discover no such unvarying system in operation when they go back to the headwaters of the Christian stream.

The variations in the New Testament accounts of the apostolic churches greatly puzzled the reformers. They assumed *a priori* that there must have been one sacred type and pattern. But when they searched the Scriptures for it they came back with different reports, like the blind men who went to "see" the elephant. It was the occasion for heart-burning disagreements in the camps of the reformers; what type of Church did the New Testament sanction? Was the Church to be guided by Bishops, or was it to be ruled by Presbyters, or was it to be a loose, fluid body, shaping all its policies from within by the action of the composite membership itself, and subject to transformation throughout the ages? All these types, and many more, were proposed in the sixteenth century and were supported by what seemed to be the plain words of Scripture. Luther followed the conservative principle that nothing in the old order of things needed to be changed unless it was found to be in positive conflict with the words of Scripture. "Whatever," he said, "is not against Scripture is for Scripture and Scripture is for it."

The more radical reformers, on the other hand, took the position that "the Church must reject in doctrine and practice everything not *positively enjoined* by Scripture." It was the Anabaptist movement, representing the common people, that carried this principle the farthest. The Anabaptists were not satisfied with reforming the historic Church; they proposed to reconstruct it root and branch, and to build it anew after the original apostolic model. They believed, in their unhistoric minds, that the old Church was "apostate," that nothing could be learned from it, that they should cut out the loop of "wilderness wanderings" which had marked the Church from the apostolic days until their own time, and they proposed to return to the New Testament pattern. The Anabaptist leaders quite naturally differed somewhat in their judgment regarding this New Testament model, but they were nearly unanimous in thinking that it was democratic in basis. They stood in the main for the "common man's" reformation, their sympathies were with the "plain people," and they found in St. Paul's churches, especially as described in the Corinthian Epistles, churches after their own hearts. Any one might "prophesy" who had a gift and could edify. Any one could govern who had a gift for government, and every one could feel that he was a pillar in the church to which he belonged. The following account of the Church, given by one of the Anabaptist leaders, is characteristic of the movement: "God's community knows no head but Christ. Teachers and ministers are not lords. . . . A true preacher would willingly see the whole community prophesy."

The peasant uprising which occurred at the very time when the Anabaptist movement spontaneously emerged at a number of widely separated localities on the Continent was an impressive sign and revelation of the contemporary hopes and expectations of the common people. The Anabaptist leaders were champions of peace and love, and they refused to take the disastrous way of violence, but they shared in full measure with the long-suffering peasants the aspirations of the human heart for freer life and wider scope. They believed and trusted that the new Church which they hoped to build for Christ and the Spirit would in the end leaven the world, transform society, and make all things new. The way to a new social order and a new State was, in their minds, through the creation of a Church according to the mind of Christ. That Church was to be the Church of the common man, and its corner stone was to be the liberty of prophesying.

If it had not been for the disorders into which some of the Anabaptist churches fell, and the fanaticism which possessed the minds of some of their leaders, particularly after they were harried to desperation by persecution, and above all, if it had not been for the wild outbreak of insanity at Münster, the democratic idea of church control and management would no doubt have made its way more effectively, and would have won a great place in the thought of that age. Even as it was, in spite of all the handicaps, Anabaptism proved to be one of the most virile and contagious of all the new religious ideals of the reforming epoch. But after the events of Münster in 1534, the name Anabaptism produced a shudder of horror in every conservative-minded person, as, once again, Bolshevism has done in our time, and from the date of Münster no one consciously adopted ideas and principles which owed their origin to that opprobrious movement.

And yet, as has happened many times before and since, with movements that have been showered with scorn and opprobrium, the conquered and defeated became in the end the conquerors. Bunker Hill is not the only instance when "a battle lost" has turned out to be "a cause won." Those very ideas and ideals that were howled down in the sixteenth century with the battle cries of a world's hate, that were crushed and beaten as the pitiless dragoons of State and Church — both Roman Catholic and Protestant — sent the exponents of these ideals in thousands to cruel forms of death, came to life again in the seventeenth century and became triumphant in the latter part of the eighteenth century, when nearly every one of the constructive principles of the Anabaptists got written into the Constitution of the United States, or got expressed in some important branch of American Christianity. Thomas Jefferson's famous sentence in his Bill for religious freedom in Virginia, "Our civil rights have no dependence on our religious opinions any more than on our opinions in physics or geometry," is a vivid, modernized form of Anabaptist ideals. "The opinions of men," Jefferson continued (meaning religious opinions), "are not the objects of civil government, nor under its jurisdiction." It is a pity the long-suffering martyrs could not have had the comfort of seeing their truth rise again and enter into its dominion.

There was a stream of refugees coming into England during the entire period of Elizabeth's reign, and among these refugees there were some Anabaptists. They are in evidence also among the immigrants even in the reign of Henry VIII. Their numbers were small; they were scattered about in various places with little cohesion, and the strong hand of authority always struck with terrific effect whenever they showed their presence as propagandists. Nevertheless, they exerted a silent influence. The ideas of the Anabaptists were in an interesting way made familiar to English readers, in fact were actually disseminated, by the publication of several books against them which appeared about the middle of the sixteenth century. This method of attack by interpretation proved to be an admirable method for the spread of their dangerous ideas. It looks almost like a clever method of advertising. The dragnets for heresy plainly reveal that Elizabethan England had many sympathizers with an Anabaptist type of Christianity.

But it is not necessary to look abroad exclusively for the origin and stimulus to dissent and separatism in England. The Lollard movement, from the days of Wyclif to the rise of the sects in the late sixteenth century, formed throughout the entire period a submerged stream of revolt against the historical Church. It was widespread, and intense with class-consciousness and with anti-church, anti-priest, and anti-sacrament feeling. It had within itself the germs of an incipient Puritanism. It also had some of the traits of the Anabaptists, and easily became a seed-bed for their views. It insisted on life and conduct rather than on form and doctrine. It disliked the baptism of children and favored unauthorized preaching and conventicle meetings. It had faith in the common man and aimed at a type of lay-religion. Here is to be found a powerful indigenous stream of dissent, and here at close hand was a native body of interest in a freer type of Christianity. Here was, too, a background of sympathy for a religion of the common people. This stream finds its headwaters both in John Wyclif and in continental Anabaptism.[1]

From 1550 onward tendencies toward separatism were strongly in evidence in many parts of England. There occurred occasional oppositions to the taking of an oath, and there were from time to time persons who denied to magistrates any right to interfere in the sphere of religion. These attitudes might have come either from the invasion of Anabaptists or from an awakened Lollardry at home. There were, too, various hidden attempts to form tiny independent religious societies, the most important of which was the Plumber's Hall congregation, organized by Richard Fitz about 1567. It was not, however, until 1581 that a full-fledged attempt was made to reconstruct the Church on a complete democratic basis. This attempt was made, not by an Anabaptist, but by Robert Browne, a scholar from Cambridge University, a first cousin to Lord Burleigh, and a man of great ability and originality. Burrage, in his valuable book *The Early English Dissenters*, says with justice that Browne was "one of the most

---

[1] See Thomas Cuming Hall's *The Religious Background of American Culture* (Little, Brown and Company, 1930).

fearless and honest religious thinkers of a great age,
who, though he himself receded from some of his
early and more bitter opinions, left therewith such
an impress on his contemporaries as to stimulate
many to similar and even more advanced views
long after he had returned to a comparatively
conservative position." [1]

Browne's first experiment in the formation of a
democratic type of church was made in the city of
Norwich with a group of men and women who already inclined to liberal "independent" views, a
number of them being Dutch emigrants living in
the diocese of Norfolk. There can be no question
that the group out of which Browne built his first
congregational church, in Norwich in 1581, was
already a "prepared" group. He did not need to
plant the congregational idea in their minds *de
novo*, for they were at heart separatists before he
came among them, and they were longing for a
leader who would share their ideal of a Church
which was to be of the people, for the people, and
by the people who composed it. For a whole generation Norwich had had a little band of men and
women who nursed in their souls the dangerous and
contagious germ of democracy.

Robert Baillie, in his *Anabaptism the true Foun-
taine* (London, 1646), says that "the Brownists did
borrow all their tenets from the Anabaptists of
old." [2] And in his earlier book, *A Dissuasive from*

[1] *Early English Dissenters*, I, 94.
[2] *Op. cit.*, p. 49.

the Errours of the Time (London, 1645), Baillie says, "The doctrine of the Anabaptists, who in great numbers fled over to England when for their Abominable and Horrible Crimes, by Fire and Water and Sword they were chased out of both the Germanies, is so like, and in many things so much the same with the Doctrine of the Brownists, that the derivation of the one from other seems to be very rational."

It does seem "rational," no doubt, to assume that the Brownist type of church was only a variant of the Anabaptist type, but it is well-nigh certain that Browne himself was wholly unconscious of being an imitator or copyist of Anabaptism. The members of his Norwich flock, however, had almost certainly been influenced by Anabaptist ideas concerning the nature of the Church. What Browne really did was to develop considerably farther than any one else had done in England the separatist principle, which was not unknown to Englishmen, and to introduce the congregational idea of a church. The practice of democratic freedom in the cities of Holland was, I am convinced, one important factor in the development of religious democracy in England. The experiences of the exiles on the Continent during the reign of Mary, the ideas and practices of the sober and respected Dutch Mennonites who had shaken themselves free from the wilder aspects of Anabaptism and, not the least, the careful study in the New Testament of the actual form of the apostolic congregations, were all formative influences toward the new idea of a church, and Browne came to his position without clearly taking account of the steps by which he arrived. Even after he had launched his first experiment in Norwich his ideas went on developing and evolving. He was probably more influenced by the congregational experiments of the Anabaptists than he himself was aware of. The democratic teachings of Althusius and, a little later, of Hugo Grotius, had a marked influence on the development of the self-government of the English churches in Holland, but their writings came too late in the century to have an influence on Robert Browne himself and these first experiments.

Browne's bold undertaking in Norwich quickly attracted unfavorable attention and brought him into conflict with the authorities of the Church. It is not possible to follow him in all the details of his suffering for his daring adventure, but it may quicken our sympathy for him to know that he was, on his own report, thrown into thirty-two prisons, "in some of which he could not see his hand at noon."[1] After a year of struggle and trial with no hope of a free opportunity for his scheme in England, Browne with a large nucleus of his church retired to Middleburg in Zealand, where the community experiment continued, and Browne's ideas took shape in three extremely important books which contain the foundation principles of early congregationalism. They are *A*

[1] Hanbury, *Historical Memorials Relating to Independents*, I, 18.

Treatise of Reformation without tarying for anie, *A Treatise on the 23 of Matthewe*, and *A Book Which Sheweth*. They were in fact three parts of one book with the covering title, *A Booke Which Sheweth the Life and Manners of all true Christians*, etc. (Middleburg, 1582).

Here we get, especially in the third section (*A Booke which Sheweth*), a profoundly democratic church system. Everything is to be regulated by the people for the benefit of the people. The people under the immediate leadership of Christ, and not the officers, constitute the Church. In fact the distinction of laity and clergy is entirely done away. Browne's definition of a church is given in *A Booke which Sheweth* as follows: "Christians are a companie of believers, which by a willing covenant made with their God, are under government of God and Christ and keepe his Lawes in one holie communion: Because they are redeemed by Christ unto holiness and happiness forever, from which they were fallen by the sinne of Adam." [1] Browne's church in Norwich had already been established on a covenant basis, and that plan of a covenant was an essential feature of all early congregational churches, including that of the Plymouth Pilgrims. The covenant idea was not new with Browne. It was Biblical in origin, and had been in operation with the Anabaptists, and also with the Puritans and the Scottish churches, long before it found expression in the church at Norwich and in Middleburg.

[1] *A Booke which Sheweth*, section A 2. The work is unpaged.

Browne was absolutely settled in his mind that magistrates, i. e. civil officers or rulers, including the sovereign of the nation, should have no control over religion. The true spiritual reformation, according to his view, must not wait for the human wisdom and guidance of those who bear civil rule. They are "blind guides" who wait for the decision of magistrates. It is a sign of anti-Christ to say, "The Kingdom of God must come by Proclamations and by Parliaments, which is 'by observation,' as though one should say, 'Loe, the Parliament, or loe, the Bishop's decrees! The Kingdom of God is within you." [1] "The magistrate's commandment must not be a rule unto me of this and that duty, but as I see it agree with the Worde of God." [2] In spiritual matters the pastor of a church has the oversight of the magistrate, not the magistrate of the pastor. The pastor is to be duly chosen and called by the church, because of his gifts for exhortation and guidance, and he holds his position solely through the action of the fellowship to which he belongs. Browne throughout his little books stands for a voluntarily supported ministry, a ministry under no bondage to tithes. He regarded the sacraments as being purely symbolic and spiritual in character. He was hostile to the keeping of special "dayes and tymes" as being "Jewish and Popish," and he disapproved of the granting of "Degrees in Theologie," since they seemed to him to be a relic of "Popish customs." His book is

[1] *Ibid.*, section A 5.   [2] *Ibid.*, section B.

practical, full of sound advice and wisdom. It is a liberal and broad-minded interpretation of the best ideas of the main-line reformers on the Continent, with certain brave unique additions. There is no sign of a mystical trait or tendency in Browne. The idea of an inward light in man, which is a notable feature of early Anabaptism, and which is still more strongly emphasized by the spiritual reformers of the same period, is wholly absent from Browne's writings and would have met a strong opposition from him, as it did usually meet from the later "Brownists." His system of thought and practice rests solidly on the "Word of God" as he had come to understand it. In this respect he belongs entirely in line with the Puritans, though in his fearless experiment with separatism he far outdistanced them.

It is not easy to settle the question why Robert Browne backslid so soon from his advanced position of leadership, became a conservative, and took the line of safety. It may be answered that he was tired of prisons and of the precarious way of life which his experiment entailed, and that he seized the path to peace and comfort as soon as it was offered. That almost certainly is not the whole of the story. There was an element of disillusionment in his hard experience as a path-breaker, and that was a factor in his decision. His brave experiment with democracy revealed, as any such early experiment with it is bound to do, that democracy is not the same beautiful thing in practice that it is in theory, in ideal, and in books.

The'ry thinks fact a pooty thing,
An' wants the banns read right ensuin';
But fact won't nowise wear the ring
'Thout years o' settin' up and wooin'.

There were sad controversies, bitter discussions, heart-breaking differences and actual divisions to face under this idealistic method. Giving all the members democratic rights did not make them all saints. Democracy is a plant of slow growth, and works well only after the patient cultivation of group spirit, the development of tests and checks and restraints on freedom, and the harmonization of *community rights* with that great, but difficult, principle of *individual rights*. We must not be too ready to belabor this chastened radical reformer and to attribute his conservative retreat solely to love of ease and desire for flesh-pots.

The next stage in the development of a church which could be called of the people and by the people was made by Henry Barrowe, who, like Robert Browne, was a Cambridge scholar, and who also, like him, was connected with those in power, being related both to Lord Bacon and less closely to Lord Burleigh. He was made of more heroic fibre, however, than was Browne. There were no dangers, no sufferings, no discouragements, and no defeats that could turn him back. He took the path of extreme hazard and went the whole way to the end of it. There was an unusual quality of nobility to the man, and his martyrdom put the final seal and crown upon his life.

He was turned from what Lord Bacon called his "vain and libertine youth" by the words of some unknown preacher in London. "Tush, shall we go hear a man talk!" his companion said as they were about to enter the preacher's church, but they went, and Barrowe came out "a changed man . . . the strangeness of which alteration made him very much spoken of," Bacon says. The second turning point of his life was his meeting with John Greenwood, another Cambridge man but of a vintage ten years later than Barrowe, the latter of Clare College, the former of Corpus Christi. Greenwood was already a separatist when they met, and he led Barrowe into the new and dangerous way. Greenwood had already thrown in his lot with a London congregation of separatists in Southwark, probably indirectly due to the influence of Browne or of his disciples, and he introduced his friend Barrowe to this congregation. Shortly after this, to be exact on the 7th of October, 1586, Greenwood was surprised while reading the Scripture at a conventicle in a friend's house in London and was imprisoned in "the Clink." Barrowe, hearing of his friend's arrest somewhat later, went to visit him in prison and was himself arrested and held without warrant. The rest of Barrowe's life and the most of Greenwood's were passed in close confinement, until April 6, 1593, when both men gave their lives on the gallows for their cause.

The thing that makes these two men so important to this particular cause is not merely that they

suffered and died for it, but that their long imprisonment gave them, especially Barrowe, many
opportunities to defend, develop, and interpret the
principles to which they were dedicated. Deprived
much of the time of light, and all the time of fresh
air, living for six years in the midst of squalor and
disease, they became, nevertheless, the most effective of all the early interpreters of the independent
and self-governing church. They wrote down their
ideas on little scraps of paper, which were copied
by their friends and secretly conveyed to Holland
and there printed in little books, largely at the risk
and expense of Robert Stokes, and put into circulation both at home and abroad. Their greatest
convert, Francis Johnson, who was to be the next
important interpreter of the democratic principle,
intercepted in Holland one of their most significant
tracts and burned the entire edition, except two
copies. He sat down to read one of them super-
ficially after the conflagration was over, and was so
powerfully impressed by its ideas that he crossed
the sea to visit the authors in prison, and eventually took up and carried on their torch when it fell
from their hands on the scaffold.

Meantime Johnson's future fellow-companion
and co-laborer, Henry Ainsworth, was "living,"
as Roger Williams says, "on ninepence a week and
upon boiled roots." John Penry also, a famous
young Puritan preacher, became convinced of their
views while they were in prison, cast in his lot with
them and went to a death similar to theirs on the

scaffold, a month after their departure. The members of the separatist church in Southwark, generally called "Barrowists," formed a project in 1597, like that of the Pilgrims twenty-three years later, to transplant their persecuted church to America — "to the country that lieth to the West in Canada." For this purpose two "merchant strangers" and one "merchant of London" made "humble suit to her Majesty to transport out of this realm divers artificers and others, *persons that are noted to be sectaries, whose minds are continually in a ferment, whereof four shall at this present sail thither in those ships that go this present voyage."* [1] The four did not reach America, but they did escape from prison and finally joined their companions in Amsterdam.

Barrowe, to return to this distinguished leader, broadened out Browne's conception of independency. He encouraged relations of sympathy, fellowship, and support between the different congregations of separatists. He introduced a degree of control and restraint over the democratic congregation by an extension of power and influence to a Council of Pastors and Elders. He, with Greenwood and his great disciple, Francis Johnson, gave the congregational principle a sound basis of advance from its simple beginnings. Like other controversialists of the period, Barrowe was too infallible-minded, too unyielding in his own opinions, too incapable of seeing any truth in the posi-

[1] Waddington's *Congregational History*, p. 114.

tion of his opponents, and he made it almost impossible for his judges to set him free by his lack of tact at moments of crisis and by his desire to pillory their errors, no matter what it might cost him. In spite of all this, Barrowe was a creative genius and is one of the real fathers of English democracy.

He pleads in his books (*A True Description out of the Word of God of the Visible Church*, 1589, and *A Brief Discovery of the False Church*, 1590) for a church that shall be a school of prophets, in which the whole Church shall exercise gifts and perform religious functions in the Spirit. He is intensely hostile to the systems of organization that have been inherited from the historical Church, and is equally dissatisfied with the church systems that the reformers have built. They have not, to his mind, "attained unto the perfect bewtie of Sion." He is, like Browne, violently opposed to the principle of giving "the civil Prince" any authority over the Christian Church. He vigorously attacks the training of ministers in the universities. Oxford and Cambridge are, to his mind, "cages full of unclean birds," and the custom of making "divines" by universities was of "popish origin," and should be suppressed as the monasteries had been! Tithes belong to an old legal dispensation, only now, he says, priests have added the tithes of "pigges and geese, which were an abomination to the Jewes." He calls creeds, even the most sacrosanct ones, unchristian inventions. He denounces the Prayer Book and the "Leitourgie." He calls

the celebration of Christmas and Easter "pagan."
He refuses all oaths, and denies that even the
Lord's Prayer should be used as a form of service.
These extreme views he shared with many of the
Puritans and with most of the sectaries of the
period. What he died for, however, was, in his own
words, the unique position that "Christ's government is tied to the whole congregation and ex-
tendeth to the action of every Christian." [1] *That*
is his holy principle.

Another one of the uncompromising principles
for which Barrowe died was the complete separation of the function of religion from the functions of
the State. Religion is to be henceforth a free and
self-chosen attitude of the soul. The congregation
which composes a given church is to be made up of
persons who are in it and of it because they have
passed over from a material to a spiritual level, not
because they were born in a certain region and are
governed by a certain national sovereign. This
spiritual attitude cannot be produced by commands. It cannot be aroused by utilitarian in-
ducements. It springs out of the soul's relations
with God, and can be a pure spiritual function only
when it is given free and full scope to develop and
mature, undisturbed by the confusions of political
policies and national interests.

We are slowly discovering that tariffs on im-
ported goods work havoc both at home and abroad
when they are determined, as they too often are,

[1] *A Brief Discovery of the False Church*, p. 223.

by political interests and are planned to benefit the constituency of a particular congressional district. Universal economic laws move in a realm above the petty councils of party leaders, and go on operating regardless of the blundering work of local politicians. The remotest countries in the world are affected by a national tariff; men and women across the globe experience tragedies or reap a harvest of profits, though they were never considered when the tariff scale was being drawn up. It is obviously a complicated task for experts, not a rôle that properly belongs to a person who has won his election by promising favors to his constituents. But even less can such a delicate personal matter as one's religious attitude toward his God be left to the votes of Parliament or the decisions of the head of a State. It is difficult for most of us now to conceive or imagine what life would be like if all our religious affairs were ordered for us by officials appointed by the State. We are inclined to assume that this free spiritual air which we breathe is an inalienable, God-given right.

It is well to be occasionally reminded that this priceless jewel of spiritual liberty has been won at terrific cost. And we shall do well to remember now that Barrowe and Greenwood and Penry were paying their part of the cost of this privilege when they climbed the scaffold in 1593. One of Barrowe's inquisitors asked him if he was ready to affirm that the Queen and the Parliament did wickedly in using their power and authority as civil magistrates to grant spiritual dominion to Bishops. "Yes," Barrowe answered, "I will write that down, by the grace of God, and I will seal it with my blood also, if so God will."

The Puritans had not yet reached this advanced position, and for a long time they continued to carry on in theory the old idea that religion must be determined, ordered, and managed from above, i. e. in the councils of State, and that ideals and attitudes of the soul of man are things to legislate about. Barrowe and his followers, whatever it might cost, would have no more to do with that ancient fallacy. Religion for them was to be an art of living, not a government policy. It was to be a source of inspiration, a way of joy and wonder, not the repetition of words and phrases that had been prepared for them at the command of the State. They materially helped by their sacrifices to make it possible for us today to choose our own art of living and to discover our own ways of joy and wonder.

The religious idea whose development I have been briefly tracing fell into good soil a little later in the counties of Lincolnshire, Nottinghamshire, and Yorkshire when it took root in the minds of a group of remarkable men in whom lay the true line of spiritual succession and transmission. As Governor Bradford puts it in his *History of Plymouth Colony,* "By the travell and diligence of some godly and zealous preachers, and God's blessing on their

labours, as in other places of their land, so in the
north parts, many became enlightened by the word
of God and had their ignorance and sins discovered
unto them, and began by His grace to reform their
lives and make conscience of their ways." Among
these leaders were John Smyth, who became pastor
of a separatist church in Gainsborough, and
Richard Clyfton, John Robinson, and William
Brewster of the famous Scrooby Church — "stern
men with empires in their brains."

They found no freedom in their northern ham-
lets and villages to work out their noble experiment, for all the forces of English society were
opposed to it, but they braved exile to find scope
for it. There was no better place in all Europe at
that date to try out their principle than in the free
cities of Holland, and there, especially in Leyden,
they not only tried it out but enlarged and expanded it, though even yet internal contentions
were harder to bear than external persecutions had
been. The exiles learned much from the tolerant
and liberal teachings that were being disseminated
in educated circles at the time. It was in 1603 that
the great work of Althusius, *Politica Methodice
Digesta*, first appeared, and this was followed not
only by new editions but by other fresh liberal interpretations of the basic principles of social organization. The leaders of the small English
churches abroad slowly absorbed new ideas and
grew in wisdom and insight. The enlargement of
vision shows at its best in John Robinson. In his

famous farewell address to the Pilgrims, he reminded them in words of extraordinary breadth that they had not yet attained the full measure of truth. God, he tells them, has yet more light to break forth out of His word. "And if God reveal anything to you by other instrument of His, be as ready to receive truth through it as ever you were to receive truth through me. . . . I beseech you to remember it; — 'tis an article of your Church covenant, — that ye be ready to receive whatever truth shall be made known unto you."

The *Mayflower* took some old colonial furniture to America that is highly prized today, but the most precious thing it took was that expectant spirit that God has more truth to break forth, and the free democratic idea of the nature of the Christian Church.

The influence of the Dutch Anabaptists upon the English exiles in Holland was a factor of prime importance for the future historical development of religious thought in England. John Smyth was one of the most important of the leaders to be captured by it. Smyth's mind was always in unstable equilibrium. He could not become fixed and static. He illustrates admirably the theory of Heraclitus that everything flows — all is process; he was always on his way to something new. He was, in spite of his mobile mind, a sound Cambridge scholar, a Fellow of Christ's College, a man of beautiful spirit. No less an authority than Bishop Creighton declared that "None of the English

Separatists had a finer mind or a more beautiful soul than John Smith." [1] His open and responsive spirit became convinced that infants were not baptized in the primitive Church and that the only true baptism was adult baptism. Under the weight of this impression, and unable to find any persons who seemed to him to be in the true apostolic succession and so commissioned to baptize, Smyth baptized himself in 1608, in other words he became a "se-baptist," a self-baptizer. He was not the first to perform this act, nor was he the last, for Holyman who baptized Roger Williams in Providence in 1638 was apparently also a se-baptist.

Smyth then baptized, or "rebaptized," his friend Thomas Helwys and a number of the exiled separatists. Even before this event occurred a group of the continental separatists had reseparated, had become Anabaptists and had joined a branch of the Mennonite Church in Holland. Smyth proposed to his group that they should all take the same course and become Mennonites, but Helwys disagreed with him and stood out for an independent organization. In the midst of the controversy Smyth died, breathing love and forgiveness to all with whom he had disagreed, and wisely declaring that he now saw that it was "a waste of time" to be fighting about "the outward Church and ceremonies."

Out of this continental defection from the sepa-

[1] *Historical Lectures and Addresses.* Quoted from Burrage, *Early English Dissenters*, I, 248. His name is spelled either way.

ratist bodies, the first Baptist church to be established in England was set up in London about 1612 under the leadership of Thomas Helwys and John Murton (or Morton). This is the beginning of what is usually called the General Baptist Society, with Arminian views. They, too, created a type of independent, self-governing church. This free, broad, liberal group of dissenters, as it spread and expanded, greatly increased the range and scope of the democratically organized churches. They soon outgrew the unsavory reputation that had attached to the Anabaptist movement, and took an important place among the dissenting forces of the Commonwealth Era.

The formation of the Particular Baptist Societies, with a Calvinistic basis, has generally been ascribed to Henry Jacob about 1616. I am convinced that Henry Jacob's church is more properly called Independent than Baptist.

To Henry Jacob apparently belongs the signal honor of being the pioneer in the formation of an independent church composed of Puritans. This independent church organized by Jacob in 1616 became the model of many more such independent churches of Puritan type. Henry Jacob had been connected with the Puritan congregation of the English Merchant Adventurers in Middleburg. As early as 1605 he wrote, in his *Principles and Foundations of Christian Religion*, that "A true Visible or Ministerial Church of Christ is a particular congregation being a spiritually perfect Corporation of Believers and having power in itselfe immediately from Christ to administer all Religious meanes of faith to the members thereof." Jacob met John Robinson in Holland about 1610, and is supposed to have been profoundly influenced by the latter, but Burrage, in his *Early English Dissenters*, has made a strong case to show that on the contrary Robinson was gradually influenced in a conservative direction by Jacob, and that they both came eventually to the view that it was possible to have nonseparatist independent churches, appointing their own ministers and governing their own congregational affairs, and yet at the same time to be unsundered in love and fellowship from the mother church. John Robinson took some such broad position as that before his death, and his followers in America advised the Massachusetts Puritans to adopt an independent congregational church system, without becoming "Separatists from the Church of England." The "Jacobite" Church of 1616 seems to have been a congregation of this new order, and consequently to have been the parent of a very important form of independency.

In any case there were always radicals in this group gathered together by Jacob who were not satisfied with such a conservative church system and who in spite of their Calvinistic outlook shared many of the ideas of the Anabaptists. In 1633 a large group of such persons separated from the "Jacobites" and established the first Particular Baptist Society. Richard Blunt, who became one of the leaders of this new branch of Baptists, and who learned the practice of baptism by immersion from the Dutch Collegiants, first introduced into England the practice of "dipping." The famous William Kiffin became a member of this group about 1638, and Hanserd Knollys was a bright light among these Baptists. These two Baptist movements proved to be extremely virile and expansive, and by the time of the Civil War had attained considerable dimensions, not only in London but in the counties as well. Here then were two more vigorous types of democratically organized churches of a congregational order, maintaining that civil magistrates have no legitimate control of religious matters.

By the beginning of the reign of Charles I the habit of forming self-governing religious societies had become contagious. All the defenders of the ancient *status quo*, from this time on, speak with horror of the growth of sectaries, and there is overwhelming historical evidence that by 1640 there were plenty of opportunities in almost every part of England for any one so disposed to become a member of some type of self-governing religious society. Edwards' estimate in 1646 of a hundred and ninety-nine sects and schisms is a manifest exaggeration,[1] but separatism, independency, seekerism and the organization of free spiritual groups

---

[1] In the first edition (1646) of the *Gangraena*, Edwards counted 176 sects and schisms. In his second edition of the same year he added twenty-three more.

around some magnetic leader or pioneer of ideas became the outstanding tendencies of the times.

One of the most novel of all the experiments in religious democracy was that inaugurated by the Society of the Quakers under the leadership of George Fox (1624–1691), the early formative years being the decade from 1647 to 1657. The original suggestion for the type of congregational meeting that emerged in the Quaker groups apparently came from the societies of Seekers which had formed in the northern counties of England, and the history of which I shall trace in the next chapter. The central idea was the complete elimination of majorities and minorities; it became the Quaker custom to reach all decisions in unity. The clerk of the meeting merely performed the function of reporting the corporate sense, i. e. the judgment of the assembled group, and of recording it. If there were differences of view, as there were likely to be in such a body, the consideration of the question at issue would proceed, with long periods of solemn hush and meditation, until slowly the lines of thought drew together towards a point of unity. Then the clerk would frame a minute of conclusion, expressing the "sense of the meeting." If unity could not be attained, then no action would be taken, or, more usually, the decision would be postponed for interim reflection and later maturing of judgment, frequently with the appointment of a committee to study the various aspects of the matters involved and propose a solution for consideration at the next session. This method, of course, called for much restraint, for humble suppression of individual impulses and, above all, for patience and meekness. It is not a method that would work well in an atmosphere of passion or prejudice, or of party spirit, but it was an admirable way to get the whole body behind the spiritual aims and concerns to which the Society was dedicated. It enabled the Quakers to proceed without voting, to eliminate the overriding of any dissatisfied minority, and it cultivated a consciousness of the importance of the group as an organ of the Spirit. Ideally the congregation included both men and women, with equality of rights and privileges, though for a long period the meetings for the affairs of the Church were conducted separately by the men and the women. This democratic method of transacting business, which originated in the English Commonwealth, has continued with considerable success for two hundred and eighty years.

These movements may perhaps seem rather unimportant from an outward aspect, while the occasions for division and for the emergence of new types often appear petty and trivial, but the experience in self-government which resulted from these small experiments proved in the total mass to be momentous, and, as we shall see, the cumulative effect upon the development of world democracy makes it a significant story in the life of the race.

III

THE SEEKER MOVEMENT

THIS chapter will deal with the birth of a unique movement in the religious life of England. In 1652 there were discovered to be numerous communities of quiet, devout people who never attended church and who nevertheless were intensely religious. They existed in large numbers in the Yorkshire dales, in the Lake district of Westmorland and Lancashire, in the western counties, and, strangely enough, in the heart of London itself. There were many thousands of these persons who had dissociated themselves from the Church, yet almost nothing has been written about them.

There have been many theories of apostolic succession during the history of Christianity. The Seekers of the Commonwealth Era held the view that the true apostolic succession is revealed only when the members of the Church, from the most exalted to the most humble, exhibit in their lives the transformed nature and the dynamic quality which characterized the original apostles. The apostles were thought of by them as high-powered men who had been raised from ordinary fishermen and tax-collectors to extraordinary saints possessed of unique moral purity, irresistible energy, a divine anointing, and a spirit-filled nature. They took these apostolic saints, glorified by time and pious imagination, as their standard of what Christian stature ought to be for everybody. What Christ had done for these men in the first century He could do, they assumed, for men and women in all centuries. To be a Christian was, in their thought, to be an apostolic person, one of a new order of humanity.

But when they surveyed the Church of their day and took stock of its membership they did not find it to be composed of saints and apostolic persons. It was made up of men and women of the common run of human nature. They were depressed by the discovery that a good deal of the old Adam remained concealed behind the fig-leaves of church membership. If Christ had lived and died to found a Church, it seemed odd to them that nothing more had come of the experiment than what they saw presented in the spiritually sterile congregations of their time. And in their disillusionment they revolted from the august church organization which had failed, took up the attitude of rebels, and set themselves to a valiant quest for a nobler type of church — the Church of the Spirit. The Seeker attitude, however, did not spring forth new-born in this period. It had had a long stage of development.

We have seen in the last chapter how powerfully the congregational movement was affected by the common man's attempt at reformation through the democratic aspirations of the Anabaptists. All the branches of Anabaptism had two ideas in common, namely to build a visible Church on the New Testament model and to "restore" the control of it to the common people.

Parallel with this movement, which is loosely nicknamed "Anabaptism," and, in fact, to a large extent growing out of it, there was another attempt at reformation and reconstruction that was even more radical and at the same time more idealistic. Historians generally refer to it as "the spiritual reformation," and its leaders in the sixteenth century are often called "spiritual reformers." They were all strongly influenced by the mystics of the fourteenth and fifteenth centuries, and all held that God and man are akin and meet as Spirit with spirit. They were the early interpreters of an inward Light in the human soul, and were forerunners of a spiritual humanism. The influence of Erasmus is fully as much in evidence in their thought as is that of the mystics. They were humanists of the noble fifteenth-century type. They were kindled and set aflame by Luther's glowing interpretation of faith — faith as interpreted in the early heroic period of the great reformer's life. And, finally, they were saturated with the New Testament revelation of God and man and the new social order for which the phrase "Kingdom of God" stood in their minds.

Hans Denck, who until recent years has been considered an Anabaptist, was the first creative interpreter of these "spiritual" ideals, though he

in turn owed a definite debt to the great radical
Thomas Münzer. Sebastian Franck, the Swabian
Chronicler, was another notable leader of the movement. Casper Schwenckfeld, Sebastian Castellio,
the French humanist, and Dirck Coornhertz, the
Dutch reformer, were some of the most important
of the Continental exponents of this ideal type of
reformation. Juan de Valdés, the noted Spanish
humanist-mystic, author of the *Christian Alphabet*
and the *Hundred and Ten Divine Considerations*, is
also one of the outstanding figures in this spiritual
movement. His *Divine Considerations* was translated into English by Nicholas Ferrar of Little
Giddings, and "Valdesso," as the English called
him, had a marked influence on George Herbert
and other saints of that period.

These spiritual reformers were all scholars of
high rank, and reveal in their writings a depth of
life and a beauty of spirit that were very rare in
that battle period of conflicting ideas. Not the
least important aspect of their teaching was their
emphasis on the gentleness and tenderness of God.
They rediscovered and proclaimed anew "the God
of Hosea." They felt that they had the beam of a
new day-spring in their souls.

The point of view which differentiates these men
most sharply from the Anabaptists, and for that
matter from all other reformers, was their emphasis
upon the supreme reality of the invisible Church
and their unconcern about the visible Church. The
visible Church seemed to them to have been a

miserable failure as an attempt to carry on through the centuries the spiritual work inaugurated by Christ in the first century. They could find no similarity between apostolic Christianity and the Church with which they were familiar. The glory of the original had, to their minds, disappeared from the world. The spirit of it was lost in the letter and in the forms. The imperial organization had smothered and killed the very truth it was intended to propagate. Contentions over creeds and sacraments and ordinations and rituals and legal forms had quite effectually defeated the central aim of Christ to propagate His life and spirit and love in the hearts of men. They turned back, therefore, to this central aim, and proclaimed *a religion of life* — the rebirth of Christ in men, and the recovery of His spirit as the spring and power of a new way of life.

Like the Anabaptists, with whom they were often confused, the spiritual reformers were met with a pitiless storm of abuse and vilification. Their little books, full of love and tenderness, were burned, their lives were harried, and they "wandered about destitute, afflicted, tormented, of whom the world was not worthy." Nothing that man could devise, however, embittered their spirit. They were tender and gentle. They remained to the end calm, serene, radiant, and triumphant. Their books are unmarred by any note of hate or contention. I have read well-nigh all of them, and have felt a sense of awe as I have lived with them

and seen the grandeur and nobility of their spirit of
love. They succeeded in their desire to belong to
the invisible Church.

Their impact on their generation was more or
less obscure, silent, and hidden. From the outside,
as a historical movement, it seemed negligible.
The authorities of Church and State thought that
they were suppressed. They never were suppressed
in fact. They produced a mild contagion among
the quiet and humble in the land that went on
spreading, though it eluded observation. Their
books were always like a secret leaven working un-
noticed and in ways that were unsuspected. Like
"Alph, the sacred river," that ran underground and
burst forth as Arethusa in a land across the sea, so
the ideas of the spiritual reformers burst forth and
had a renewal of life across the Channel in England.
Even as early as 1560 John Knox refuted a book
which, he said, "written in the english tongue doth
contein the lies and the blasphemies imagined by
Sebastian Castalio." [1] The little books by Denck
and Franck and Castellio continued to drift into
England throughout the reign of Elizabeth. They
occasionally laid their influence upon the English
exiles abroad, in cases where these exiles were
open-minded, and some copies came across into
England when the exiles returned. Some copies,
again, came in from Holland whenever Dutch
sectaries succeeded in migrating and finding a
home. John Everard and his disciples from the

[1] *The Confutation of the errours of the careless by necessitie.*

time of James I became the main purveyors in England of the ideals of these spiritual reformers. He reproduced in English the substance and the spirit of the men who in the midst of hate and scorn and bitterness had essayed to build an invisible Church.

Everard was an excellent scholar, a Cambridge doctor of divinity. He translated into English Hans Denck's *Confession of Faith*, Sebastian Franck's *The Tree of Knowledge of Good and Evil*, the *Mystical Divinity* of Dionysius the Areopagite, and *The Divine Pymander* (i. e. Poemander) of Hermes Trismegistus. Everard, in conjunction with his disciple Giles Randall, appears also to have translated a part of the *De Visione dei* of Nicholas of Cusa, and the *Theologia Germanica* from the Latin edition by Sebastian Castellio. Everard and Randall together by their writings and translations did much to put the ideas of the Continental spiritual reformers into circulation in England before the beginning of the Commonwealth.

There are three translations in manuscripts in the Cambridge University Library ascribed to Dr. John Everard. The first is called *The Letter and the Life, or the Flesh and the Spirit*. It is the translation in fourteen chapters of Franck's *Von dem Baum des Wissens Gutes und Böses*. The second is *Germane Divinity: A Golden Book*, "translated into Latin out of high Dutch by John Theophilus" (Castellio) and into English by Everard in 1628.

There is a page out of "ye workes of John Tau-lerus," and two chapters of Nicholas of Cusa's *Vision of God*. Giles Randall in his own name translated the *De Visione dei* in 1646 with the title *The Single Eye or the Vision of God*, and in 1648 he published his own translation of Castellio's edition of *Theologia Germanica*, which differs materially from that of Everard. He also translated out of Latin under the title *A Bright Starre*, in 1646, the *Third Part of the Rule of Perfection by a Capuchin Friar*.

Everard, moreover, was one of the most vital preachers in London during the reigns of James I and Charles I. It was during this period of his preaching that the Seeker movement was born in England.

The first and most marked characteristic of the Seeker, both in England and on the Continent, was his disillusionment over *the authority and power of the visible Church*. The Church in our day has been under fire from many quarters, and some persons with unhistoric minds have supposed this broadside attack to be a new feature of this age and a peculiar sign of modern perversity. It is by no means novel, nor does it of necessity indicate perversity. These Seekers three hundred years ago were among the most intensely religious people in the world, and yet they concluded that the days of the visible Church were ended, its power exhausted, its creeds and sacraments unefficacious, its ministry futile. Like so many other positions that were held in England at the time of the Commonwealth, this same conclusion regarding the Church was reached on the Continent a hundred years earlier. Sebastian Franck in his *Chronicle* in 1536 records that "Some desire to allow Baptism and other ceremonies to remain in abeyance till God gives another command — sends out true labourers into His harvest — some have, with great desire, a longing for this and desire nothing else." That indicates that already in Luther's day there were persons who felt that the old church systems had come to an end, and that no new Church could be organized until there should be an unmistakable fresh "command" from God to inaugurate it. Already there were some who were intensely longing for that command to be sent forth and who took the attitude of "waiters" or "seekers."

Franck's account proceeds as follows: "Some others agree with those, who think the ceremonies since the death of the apostles are equally defiled, laid waste and fallen — that God no longer heeds them and does not desire that they should be longer kept, on which account they will never again be set up, but Christians are now to proceed entirely in the Spirit and in Truth and never in an outward manner."

This last passage expresses the attitude of the spiritual reformers. For them the outward symbols had come to an end, the function of the visible Church was over, and Christianity was thought henceforth to be an inward life and a spiritual power, revealed in individual persons, whereas the characteristic expectation of the Seeker was for a new Church to be built under a new apostolic dispensation, inaugurated by God.

Ubbo Phillips, who was a fellow-laborer with Menno Simons in the sixteenth century, in his Confession of Faith, makes a similar statement to that of Franck's. He declares that there were little groups of Christians on the Continent in his day "who served God in quiet simplicity — after the manner of the patriarchs; who sought God from the heart and who served Him and clave to Him without preachers, teachers or outward gatherings." [1] These groups of which Ubbo Phillips wrote might be of either of the above types. In any case they were persons who were done with the existent Church and had withdrawn from it, since they felt that it was no longer able to supply them with a religion of life and power — a religion of the Spirit.

The earliest mention I have found in England of disillusionment about the authority of the Church is in Henry Barrowe's *A Brief Discovery of the False Church* (1590). He says: "There are already those in England who teach that the Church of Rome is no true Church, its ordinations and sacraments are ineffective, its ministry is void, but the original seed of the Anglican Church received baptism and ordination from 'that false Church,' therefore they say that its ministries (the Anglican) and its baptisms are void and empty." [2]

[1] Quoted from Barclay's *Inner Life of the Religious Societies of the Commonwealth*, p. 174.

[2] *Op. cit.*, pp. 99–112. Given in substance in the text.

This is an early pre-Seeker position. The dilemma which confronted the serious Christian at this point was the absence of any one authoritatively commissioned to ordain or baptize. Barrowe proceeds to express the difficulty which confronted those who have made this discovery: "They say that all extra-ordinarie offices of the Church have ceased and so must all the building of Christ's Church cease, and the work of this ministrie cease until some second John the Baptist, or new apostles, be sent from heaven, except peradventure they, after their long travail, bring forth some new Evangelist: and surely if they make a new ministrie they must also make a new gospel and confirm it with new miracles." That passage gives, already as early as 1590 in England, the full-fledged Seeker position. There is no authoritative Church, no outward ordination, baptism, or ministry, nor can any such be set up effectively until there is a new apostolic dispensation which demonstrates itself with miraculous power.

A similar view is given in 1619 by a devoted Puritan Scholar who was already not far off from the Seeker position. John Wilkinson, in his *An Exposition of the Thirteenth of Revelation* (London, 1619), says in regard to the confusion of the times: "I deny not but there are many amongst them that are the Saints and Servants of Christ, that are godly and zealous people. . . . Such persons, I say, are fit stones for the building of the Church of Christ but so long as they remain in this confusion

they can no more bee the true visible Church of
Christ than a heape of stones fitted for a building
can be said to be a house; therefore they must be
separated from the wicked and placed together
according to the order prescribed by Christ Jesus
and practised by his Apostles in the New Testament before they can be so esteemed."

It will be illuminative to turn as a comparison to
a contemporary description of the Commonwealth
Seekers written in 1655. William Allen, in his
book *A Doubt resolved or Satisfaction for the Seekers*
(1655), describes Seekers exactly as Barrowe does.
"They make [he says] a considerable obstacle in
their way of coming into Church-communion,
Gospel ordinances, viz., the want of a right ad-
ministrator: For they suppose that since that general apostasy, from the purity of faith and Gospel
order which befel the Churches, upon the entering
of the Papacie into the world, there hath none
appeared sufficiently authorized by God to rally
again what had been routed by the hand of the
enemy, or to gather Churches or to administer
Ordinances; all due Administrators in this kind
being perished from the earth, and that therefore
we must be content to *wait* until God shall raise up
some such, whose authority in this behalf he shall
attest with visible signs of his presence, by gifts of
the Holy Ghost, and divers miracles as at the first
erection of Gospel Churches and ordinances." [1]

The author shows, however, that there is another

[1] *Op. cit.*, p. 14.

type of Christian, more or less linked up with Seekers, who believe themselves to be above ordinances and to have no need of them. He says that "there are many in these times who, to render water baptism unnecessary, do construe most of the Scriptures which speak of baptism as meant of the baptism of the Spirit . . . who do interpret those words I Corinthians 12:13 'By one spirit we were all baptized into one body' to be meant of the baptism of the Spirit, to be incorporated visibly into this one body of Christ which is his Church, by vertue of being baptized with the Spirit, whether they have ever received water baptism or not."

John Saltmarsh, who is one of our best and clearest guides for light on the nature and character of the Seekers, says in his *Groanes for Liberty* (London, 1646) that they form a well-known existing sect in his day, and claims for them an honorable place in the spiritual movements of the time. "Seekers," he writes in the second part of the above Tract, "question the way of the Church and of Ordinances, as Baptism, etc. because they find the *power* was first given to the *Apostles* with gifts [i. e. tongues and miracles] and from *them* to others, but they [the Seekers] dare not take it from Anti-Christ and the Bishops [of Rome], as the Reformed Kingdoms generally take it, nor from the Churches [of the Separatists] because they find no such power begun from the Churches." [1]

[1] The second part of Saltmarsh's work is called "The Beam of Light." The quotation is from p. 23.

The two somewhat diverse positions which Allen presents appear and reappear wherever we can trace the Seeker movement in England. Those who felt the need of an outward organization were waiting and seeking for some one to come with an apostolic commission to inaugurate once more a visible Church with divine gifts and with spiritual power like the primitive one. Others of these Seeker groups who were more mystically minded were convinced that the visible Church was no longer needed in the world. The dispensation of outward performances had for them come to an end. The dispensation of the Spirit had begun. Everything henceforth that has to do with religion is to be inward. To be a Seeker of this second type was to be a person who waited and sought for the demonstration and power of the Spirit, revealed within the soul. Organization for them was a mark of weakness and a return to "beggarly elements."

The one-sided and inadequate feature of this movement is, of course, obvious to any modern mind. We know, with our broadened historical insight, that spirituality cannot be disembodied, nor can it be cut apart from some kind of forms and organizations. An invisible Church without any incarnation in a visible one would almost certainly soon become not only "invisible" but ineffective as well. That point, however, need not lessen our appreciation of these seventeenth-century venturers.

It can, I think, be shown historically that the

Seekers deserted the Church not because they had lost their religion and had become apostate in faith and life: the real trouble was that their expectation of what the spiritual stature of a Christian ought to be had traveled so far ahead of the actual spiritual stature which the Church was producing that they refused to recognize *that* Church as Christ's spiritual organ. William Penn has given us a vivid picture of their attitude in his Preface to the *Journal of George Fox*. They left, he says, "all visible Churches and societies and wandered up and down as sheep without a shepherd, and as doves without their mates; seeking their Beloved."

One of the most baffling historical problems connected with this epoch is the discovery of the origin and development of the actual societies of Seekers, which are known to have been in existence in many parts of England by 1650, especially in the northern counties. Did the movement have a founder? If so, who was he? Was it indigenous, or did it originate abroad and migrate to England? If it came from the Continent, when did it originate there and what place was its native habitat? Barclay, in his epoch-making study of the religious societies of the English Commonwealth, was convinced that the original Seeker societies were Dutch, and had their beginnings in a branch of the Mennonites.

I think I have successfully shown, in my *Spiritual Reformers of the Sixteenth and Seventeenth Centuries*, that the organized groups of Dutch Seekers known as "Collegiants" or "Rhynsburgers" did not come into existence before 1619, while the famous Amsterdam Collegium or Society did not begin until 1645. I have been unable to find evidence of the existence of any definite Seeker groups in Holland before the earlier date (1619). Disillusionment about the validity of the Church had existed, as we have seen, in many places in almost all European countries since the beginning of the Reformation. This disillusionment was far more serious, even more tragic, than my merely casual reference to it would indicate. There were times in Luther's life when he was almost overwhelmed with a haunting sense that the reformation of the Church was effecting no real change in men's lives. After all the turmoil and contention, the fierce strife and costly division of forces, there often seemed to him to be no new dynamic in operation. The new Church, in his moments of depression, appeared to be as devoid of power as the old one had been. Changing names and terms and phrases did not alter the hard and solemn facts of life. Luther, for his own relief, charged the seeming defeat to the renewed activity and desperate maliciousness of Satan, who thought he saw his power slipping away and consequently had aroused himself for a terrific last-line death grapple. Calvin and Knox and the other reformers went through similar periods of disillusionment, though they were not so profound and depressing as Luther's were. The staggering fact that confronted them all in their sober reflections was the slight moral and spiritual alteration that had occurred in the actual lives of church members.

These pillar reformers, with their intense convictions, did not incline to attribute the lack of operative power to the invalidity of the new church organizations. They seldom had doubts respecting the efficacy of the reformed sacraments or the authoritative character of the reformed ministry. They all believed that they had the warrant and seal of the Word of God for each step that had been taken toward reformation. But there were other men of sound scholarship and of as undoubted spiritual insight who did not feel that assurance. They inclined, on their part, to attribute the obvious lack of moral and spiritual power to failure to discover the right reforming principle and the true basis for church reorganization. Persons of this type were as cold and dubious toward the new reformed Churches as they were toward the ancient Church. They found no basis of validity in any of them and no mark of primitive apostolic power. They took the attitude of "waiters" or "desirers" in reference to the building of the visible Church. They would "wait" until God himself should reveal a plan for a Church that would be adequate for Christ's spiritual mission in the world, and in the meantime — the *interim period* as Coornhertz called it — they would "seek" for light and guidance to become quiet, living members of the invisible Church. This attitude of mind, this tendency of thought, prevailed wherever the writings of the spiritual reformers had made converts and disciples. But before 1619 one finds only scattered

individuals who quietly nursed an unformulated
attitude in these matters, not a definite revolt from
the Church nor a break with its age-old forms and
customs. The formation of the first "Collegium"
in Rhynsburg marks, in my judgment, the rise of
Seekers on the Continent as a specific movement.
Before that time there was no coherent body of
ideas to be propagated, nor was there any organized society that could undertake the work of
propagation.

That date (1619) is obviously too late to enable
us to trace the origin of English Seekers to the influence of Dutch exponents and interpreters of
the Seeker ideas. In any case there is no need to
search for an outside influence to account for the
birth of the English Seeker movement during the
first quarter of the seventeenth century, when it
actually arose. In so far as there was any outside
influence at all, it is to be found in the quickening
power of the writings of the early spiritual reformers, especially Denck, Franck, Schwenckfeld, Castellio and Valdés, whose books were certainly in
the hands of awakened English preachers as early
as the reign of James I. During the period of that
reign the royal attempt to stiffen and harden the
authority of the Church, and to make its claim and
sway uniform for the nation, resulted in a greater
spread of the disillusionment to which I have referred and which was already strongly in evidence,
as we now know, by the year 1590. The impact of
vital books from the Continent on the spirit of men

of this type quickly produced a little band of fearless spiritual "prophets" to whose kindling lives
and words the Seeker movement of the time was
due.[1]

I shall turn, directly, to speak of some of these
English spiritual prophets. But for the moment
I want to emphasize the point that the English
Seekers had no "founder" in the proper sense of
the word. The Seeker movement, at least in the
early stages of it, was a state of mind rather than a
well-organized and directed body of people. It was
a widespread tendency of thought, a drift of ideas
that were more or less highly charged with emotion. It was a cumulative tendency that had been
slowly gaining adherents ever since, for one reason
or another, doubts had begun to spread about the
validity of the existing Church order, and ever
since serious souls had raised questions about the
power and authority of ordination and the sacraments. This cumulative tendency had been fur-
thered even more by the growing sense in many
minds that nothing that had yet been done in the
way of reformation had brought any new spiritual
dynamic into operation that demonstrated itself in
the transformation of human lives and human society. Persons who were in that state of mind were
to be found in every branch of English Christianity
in the early years of James' reign, and we need not
be surprised that persons who were thus minded

[1] I am using the word "prophet" to denote an effective and powerful exponent and interpreter.

gradually dissociated themselves from the churches and formed coherent groups of Seekers.

I am now ready to turn to a brief consideration of some of the most notable spiritual prophets, as I have called them, who developed this state of mind, brought it to white heat, and transmitted it to the little bands of devout disciples who formed the far-flung Seeker groups of the Commonwealth. I shall deal mainly with four men who, I am convinced, were the most vital creators in England of such a state of mind.

I shall speak first of Dr. John Everard, to whom I have already alluded. He is, I feel sure, the father of the movement. More than any other man in England Everard absorbed the central teaching of the Continental spiritual reformers, appropriated these principles and made them his own through personal experience, became himself a dynamic spiritual organ, and, set aflame with burning light and truth, made a host of converts. William Penn refers three times to Everard in his printed *Works*. He calls him "that renowned Independent," "that great spiritual separatist," "that notable and very religious man." Rapha Harford, in his Dedicatory Epistle to Oliver Cromwell, in the first edition of Everard's *Some Gospel-Treasures Opened* (1653), writes: "Of this Author we may say, he was one who sought after Wisdom and found it." He adds: "He would often say that he desired to be acquainted with men who had experience with Christ rather than men of notions and speculations,

[with men] *that desired to act rather than to talk.*"
Harford, speaking as a contemporary, makes the
comment that Everard steered "his way clear between . . . the Rationalist who wants to square out
God according to his own Reason, or else he is no
God," and, on the other hand, the high flown antinomian who "has quite left all Religion behind and
by degrees hath turned licentious Ranter."

The central strain of Everard's preaching was
his continual insistence that Christianity does not
lie in outward organizations, external performances, historical knowledge, Scriptural phrases,
repetition of pious words, or a slavish obedience
to the Letter, but rather a personal experience of
the life and power of Christ revealed within the life
of man as a spiritual reality. Everard is essentially a mystic, and belongs in the group of persons
who will be dealt with in the next chapter, but he
no less clearly was a major influence in spreading
disillusionment in regard to all visible churches and
in his powerful appeal to start building forthwith
the invisible Church, the Church of the Spirit.
There is no doubt in the mind of one who reads
Everard's sermons that he himself was "a happy
finder," that there was a vital dynamic operating
in his life, but the effect of his preaching was to set
serious-minded persons on a quest for *the substance
of religion.*

In this respect he produced a harvest of Seekers
who could not rest content with the dry husks of
an outward religion. As often happens, so here

once more, the "finder" stimulated others to become "seekers." Most Christians in his time, Everard thinks, are busy "playing with cockelshells and pebble-stones that lie on the outcoasts of the Kingdom," and have not yet launched out into the deep with God, but this brave soul, who was so often in prison that King James suggested that his name should be changed from Everard, which means "Ever-out," to Neverard, i. e. "Never-out," helped many to take the risks and the ventures of exploring the open ocean with all its perils.

Roger Brierly (or Breirly), "minister of the Gospel at Grindelton," is another one of the "spiritual prophets" who sowed the seed for the harvest of Seekers that followed. Grindleton is situated at the foot of Pendle Hill, — George Fox's Mount of Vision, — and forms the frontier of the northern Seeker region. Brierly's disciples were dubbed "Grindletonians" by the heresy hunters. Stephen Denison, in *The White Wolfe* (London, 1627), says: "I would we had not Grindletonian Familists in the north parts of England, who hold (among other things) that we must not now goe by motives but by motions [i. e. inward guidances] and that when God comes to dwell in a man He so fills the soule that there is no more lusting" (p. 39).[1] Brierly also was included in Archbishop

[1] Thomas Comber, in *Christianity no Enthusiasm* (1678), says that there were "Grindletonian Familists" "in the north parts of England" and that "Hell broke loose there." These and some others were "sucked in by the Quakers," p. 5.

Laud's blacklist. The Archbishop in 1641 charges that "one Brierly and his Independent Congregation are of the belief that 'the Child of God in the power of grace,' doth perform every duty so well that to ask pardon for falling, either in matter or manner, is a sin."[1] The charge is, of course, intended to show that the Grindletonians profess a type of holiness which is antinomian. The Archbishop of York had already in 1628 publicly examined Brierly on the same charge, and on forty-nine others, and had found him innocent. Archbishop Laud should have known, one would think, of the decision of the Court at York.

Roger Brierly was born at Marland, near Rochdale, in 1586, of an excellent family. He was probably educated at Rochdale in Archbishop Parker's famous grammar school, and was trained under the spirit-stirring ministry of Joseph Midgley. Both Joseph Midgley and his greater father, Richard, were strongly dissenting Puritans.[2]

There had already for a generation been an intensely religious atmosphere here in this region of the West Riding.

In the near-by town of Sedbergh, Giles Wigginton, a popular and beloved preacher, was suspended and imprisoned for his dissenting Puritan teaching and his advanced, liberal ideas.[3]

[1] Laud's *Works* in "Anglo-Catholic Library," VII, 132.
[2] *Journal of Nicholas Assheton*, edited by F. R. Raines (1848), and Robert Halley's *Lancaster, its Puritanism and non-Conformity* (1869).
[3] *The Second Part of a Register*, edited by Albert Peel (Cambridge, 1915), II, 238–255.

Brierly's life work was mainly done in the parish of Grindleton. His preaching was extraordinarily effective, his influence was widespread, and there is plain evidence that he left in the region round about a large following of persons more "advanced" than himself, and there seems to have been "something of personal magnetism about the man." [1] He left behind a large collection of sermons and many poems in manuscript. The sermons and many of the poems were published in Edinburgh in 1670, in a volume entitled *A Bundle of Soul-convincing, Directing and Comforting Truths*. "The Epistle to the Reader" is signed by J. C.,[2] who bears the testimony that Roger Brierly "spoke in the authority and power of the living God until the Seed of God was brought forth by the Spirit of life in open view in men's hearts." The sermons themselves confirm that contemporary testimony. Dr. Theodor Sippell, who first directed my attention to Brierly, thinks that his religious position is that of a pronounced Lutheran with his central emphasis on faith. I cannot agree with this judgment. I find Brierly's writings saturated with the attitudes and insights

[1] William Self Week's *Clitheroe in the Seventeenth Century* (1927), p. 175. Archbishop Laud, in the passage already referred to, says that "one Spissberrye, yet living and of that Independent fraternity (the Grindletonians) maintains that God works all things in us and we are but organs, instruments and empty trunks."

[2] In the Catalogue of the British Museum "John Cheney" is suggested as the J. C. Dr. Theodor Sippell in his *Zur Vorgeschichte des Quäkertums* (1920) proposes John Camm, the Seeker and Quaker, for J. C., which is extremely improbable.

of the spiritual reformers. He has all the marks of
being a gentle disciple of John Everard, though he
is only eleven years younger. His preaching, like
Everard's, would tend to make men Seekers, as it
apparently did. Alexander Gordon, in his article
on Brierly in the *National Dictionary of Biography*,
says quite rightly that "Brierly's spirit reminds
one of Juan de Valdés." Nicholas Ferrar's translation of the writings of Valdés did not appear until
1638, and I know of no earlier translation, but
Brierly must have known the writings of some of
the spiritual reformers either from Everard or from
some other source.

Brierly's constant criticism of dependence on
"the Letter" or on "notions" or on "heady opinions" is very typical, and he frequently calls his
hearers to a religion of the heart, of the life, or
power, "the Religion of Christ," as the first sermon
expresses it, a religion that "puts the crosse at the
centre of life." "No one," he says (*op. cit.*, p. 18),
"ever knows Christ without walking on foot with
Him in His death and miserie." He is everywhere
against a "forensic Christianity" that ends in
"conceit of knowledge" and an external, theoreti-
cal point of view. It is, he says, as though we
should "know" a country by reading books and
studying maps about it "without ever going there."
"Christ came, not to set men disputing about opinions." "Divinity stands not in curious searching
of hidden things, but in plain evidence of truth
that pierces the heart." "The Word of Truth is a

mighty Word and opens to man the book of his own heart." "All high-flying religion is not of Christ." "What then, are all those high contemplations that soar above and seek Christ in heaven and make Him a high speculative Angel and rack their thoughts and beat their brains in comprehending? when alack! He is with us, like us, suffering, watching, praying, poor, judged and reproached, dying as we are" (p. 112). "The Gospel is soft, lowlie and tender."

He reveals a sensitiveness and tenderness like that of John Woolman, of which the following passage is a sample: "These (word-notion) Christians are still hard hearted men, had rather the poor perish in the streets than they want to satisfie their appetites: For if a man would spare the tenth penny that he spends idelie, only to please his lusts would it not relieve a Town? Nay, if that vain waste were spared, which man spends on his lusts [i. e. pleasures], it would keep the poor of a Paroch [parish]. And then if our garish women would but spare one Lace and garde of five, it would clothe them [the poor] from the cold. Well, Christ will be no pattern for these things." "Brownbread and the Gospel is good fare" (p. 9). He has obviously outgrown the Church of his time and shaken himself free of its creeds and ritual, and he holds loosely and feebly to external sacraments. He boldly declares that "Bread and wine are silly things where the heart is not led further" (p. 96). His poetry is second-rate, but it reveals as clearly as his sermons

do that he is done with "Rudiments" and is ready
to "venture neck or nothing" for a full-blown religion of the Spirit. Brierly was arrested in 1628 on
charges of heresy, and was imprisoned in York
while waiting to be tried in the Archbishop's Court.
Fifty errors of belief were charged against him.[1]
The motion against him and the type of charges
that were formulated would indicate that his
preaching had produced, as early as 1628, a widespread popular defection from the Church in that
region, with strong Seeker tendencies, a weakening
of adherence to forms and outward systems, and an
eager quest for an experience of the Spirit. The
fiftieth charge is a revealing one: "There is as
much difference between Mr. Bryerly's preaching
and other men's as between salvation and damna-
tion, and a wicked man may do as much as most
men preach and may obey all the written word and
yet be damned."

I am convinced that Brierly and his Grindletonians furnish us with a positive clue to the origin
of the Seeker Societies in the Yorkshire dales.

But our third "spiritual prophet" brings us still
closer to the trail that leads on straight into the

[1] Two different copies of these charges exist in MS in the Bodleian
Library, entitled "Certain eroneous opinions gathered from the mouth
of Mr. Bryerly and some of his hearers" (Cod. Rawl. D. 1347, fol. 301).
The "opinions" charged against him are far more extreme in position
than his views expressed in his sermons indicate. Some of his followers
may possibly have gone farther than he did in the direction of anti-
nomianism, but it is probable that the "charges" are heavily colored
by the "reporters." In any case Brierly was exonerated and was invited to preach in York Minster before he returned to Grindleton.

camp of the Seekers. This is John Webster of
Clitheroe, also, like Grindleton, at the foot of
Pendle Hill. He was ordained a priest by Morton,
Bishop of Durham, about 1634 or a little earlier,
and became curate at Kildwick-in-Craven that
same year.[1] The year following he had a transforming experience from which he ever afterwards
dated his "new life." In describing his transformation he says, "The Lord in his mercy hath cleared
my spirit from these mists" — "these mists" referring to dependence on wit, argument, human
learning, contention, strife, and carnal weapons.
He made the discovery, in short, that true religion
is an inner spring of life and power. It seems pretty
clear that the transforming experience was due to
the impact of a body of new ideas which were received either from some living person or through
books. It may very well have been the direct influence of Roger Brierly, who was still living at the
time, as he died at Burnley in 1637.

In 1643 Webster was master of the grammar
school in Clitheroe. He studied medicine at some
period of his life and acted as surgeon in Colonel
Shuttleworth's regiment. He was also for a period
chaplain in the Parliamentary Army. He was appointed vicar of Mitton in 1648, where he remained
until 1652, during which period he sometimes
preached at Grindleton nearby, always without pay
— "gratis," the account says. It is doubtful if he
took a salary for preaching at any time after his

[1] Weeks, *Clitheroe in the Seventeenth Century.*

"experience" occurred. In 1653 he wrote: "Did ever Christ teach you to preach for hire and to make contracts how much you must have for exercising that ministry?" [1] He preached a remarkable series of sermons in Allhallows Church, London, in 1654, while temporarily engaged upon "some employment in the Lord's work in this great city." He had a most distinguished audience during the London period of preaching, and was at least once invited to preach at Whitehall. The last years of his life were spent quietly in Clitheroe, where he died in 1682.

Either before or after his "great experience" he extensively read and studied the mystics and the spiritual reformers. He shows an acquaintance with the writings of Plato and Plotinus, "Dionysius," Paracelsus, Cornelius Agrippa, Ficino, Mirandola, Valentine Weigel, Van Helmont, and Jacob Boehme. His sermons give the impression that John Everard had influenced him more profoundly than any one else, and he finishes his last collection of sermons — *The Liberty of a Christian is in his own Breast* — with two pages of warm appreciation of Everard. His pet phrases and favorite texts are much the same as those which appear and reappear in *Some Gospel-Treasures Opened*.

Webster is far more explicitly a Seeker than either Everard or Brierly, though he is merely carrying their points of view farther, and making

[1] *The Saint's Guide.*

the challenge to the Church a bit more robust. "The Church," he cries out, "what is that, think you? Without question the meaning of the Apostle is not to be taken literally of a material Church; nor 'tis not meant of a congregation of men and women assembled or congregated together (as the wisest men take it); for this in the Scripture sense is not called a Church, much less in a low and vulgar Acceptation of a Meeting place, built of Bricks or Wood or Stone: But the Church is the Temple of God, the House of God, the Body of Christ" [1] — i. e. it is an invisible Church. All his religious emphasis is on inward experience, divine anointing, spiritual preparation, and he everywhere discounts the value of the outward, far more in fact than can be safely done: "Thou mayst have a notion and an opinion of the things of God, and thou hast them by History and by Relation or Education or Example or Custom or Tradition — *but if thou hast no evidence of Christ's mighty miracles and Godlike power in thine own soul, how canst thou be a witness or say that thou hast seen* and heard?" [2] He proceeds to say in the same sermon: "Thou hast joined thyself here and there and gone from one Church-society to another. . . . I have joined myself to the Presbyterians and I have found their way too short, it would not do; I have come over to the Independents and thought that way seemed a better and more refined way, yet it is too narrow,

[1] *The Saint's Guide*, p. 84.
[2] *The Saints Perfect Freedome*, p. 239.

I cannot wrap myself in that covering. . . . Then say the Anabaptists come over to us and we will give thee satisfaction; we have the true Baptism, none so near the Word of God as we. But when thou hast done all these things *to find rest* and to quench the fire that began to burn in thee. . . . Dost thou think there is anything of Christ in all this? Is it not to run away and turn thy back on Christ and to live by thy wits and invention?" "Stand in the Light of God and there rest quiet, this is the way of life, this is Christ's way." [1]

Here Webster has gone all the way over to the disillusionment of the Seekers in reference to the visible Church, but he gives the impression that he has already "found" the source of inward life and joy and power and so, too, had many others of those who called themselves Seekers.[2]

In 1635 Webster had a profound religious experience which "cleared his spirit of mists." He had apparently about this time come under the liberating influence of Roger Brierly. For the next fifteen years he was an effective preacher of liberal views, usually preaching without pay, since he appears to have held it wrong to accept a salary for preaching. He seems to have gone all the way over to the

---

[1] *The Saints Perfect Freedome*, pp. 243–246.

[2] William Prynne, in *A Fresh Discovery of some Prodigious New Wandring, Blasing Stars and Firebrands* (1645), speaks of "Those Independent Seekers, who like wandering Stars, gad about every day after New Lights, New Fashions of Church Government, wavering like empty clouds without water." But by no means did all the Seekers "gad" and "waver."

Seeker position, and that, too, in the very region where a little later Seekers were most numerous.

Webster attacks "academick" and "scholastick" training as a preparation for ministry even more fiercely than did George Fox. He says in a memorable sentence: "If the quintescence of all humane learning were, as a magisterial extract, monopolized in one man, yet were it no fit qualification for a minister of the Gospel." (!) [1] He calls "Academick and Scholastick Learning" "the rotten rubbish of Babylonish Ruins," while "the Wit, Reasons and Collected Notes from Orthodoxical Authors" he calls "rotten crutches to support Lameness." He is as hot against what he calls "man-made ministers" as any early Quaker ever was. As we have seen, he is opposed to a paid ministry, to ministry as a profession, or "Trade," as he calls it. He sees no true place for any kind of forms or ceremonies or set methods. He reckons all sacraments as "Types and Shadows," "outward Rules, Forms and Carnal Ordinances." Those who try to construct organizations and external systems are all "Babel-builders" or "Idolmakers," and are in "the elementish" stage. In "An address to all those that set up forms and external Worship instead of the spiritual life," he tells them that "no form of external Worship and Discipline (though never so near the model that you may imagine is laid down in the Letter of the Scriptures) doth make a saint where the life and

[1] *The Saint's Guide*, p. 7.

power is absent." This is thoroughly in the characteristic manner of the Seeker.

It is no wonder that after 1652 Webster was often charged with being a Quaker, as before that date he had been called by almost every other opprobrious label of the epoch. He never, in spite of his close approach, became a Quaker. He was critical of the Familists and did not feel at home with them. He belongs truly and properly with the Seekers of the spiritual type. He had gone beyond the existing Churches, as he knew them, and was "waiting" for some community way of life that would offer complete liberty for the cultivation and exercise of a religion of the Spirit. We may take as our last word from him this testimony: "It is not outward profession or conformity that counts, but Christ in you. . . . It is the incoming of the power of God in our spirit by which alone our Freedom, Deliverance and Salvation is wrought." [1]

Here then, was another powerful life and voice crying for a whole generation on the edge of the Seeker region, where, in 1652, George Fox found "a prepared people, waiting to be gathered." In the light of this situation it is no wonder that Fox was powerfully attracted by the pull of Pendle Hill.

The consummate flower of the Seeker movement was, to my mind, John Saltmarsh, a third John and, like the other two, a "beloved disciple" of spiritual liberty. We will briefly consider him.

[1] *The Saints Perfect Freedome*, pp. 235–237.

Saltmarsh was born in Yorkshire toward the end of the reign of Queen Elizabeth. He received the degree of M.A. at Magdalen College, Cambridge, some time, probably ten years, before 1640. He was for a period rector of Heslerton in Yorkshire, but resigned his living there in 1643, on account of his scruples against taking tithes for preaching. From this time until his death in 1647 he was one of the most impressive interpreters of pre-Quaker ideas in England, ideas that are best called "Seeker principles." The last year of his life he was an army chaplain, and had a large place with the soldiers, as Richard Baxter regretfully admits. Saltmarsh shows a strong mystical strain, both in his life and in his writing, and I shall refer to him in that connection in the next chapter. At present I am concerned only with his Seeker views.

He describes Seekers in each one of his books, *Sparkles of Glory*, *Groanes for Liberty*, *Reasons for Unitie*, *Smoak in the Temple*, *Some Drops of the Viall*, and *Beam of Light*, and always with sympathy for their spiritual aims and aspirations, in a way that makes one feel that he is identified with them. He says in *Sparkles of Glory* (p. 292), "The Seekers wait onely in prayer and conference, pretending to no certain determination of [outward] things, nor any infallible consequences or interpretation of Scripture." Like John Webster and George Fox, Saltmarsh insists that true ministers can be made only by "the call and unction of the Spirit . . . for surely it is not a University, a Cam-

bridge or Oxford, a Pulpit and black Gowne or
Cloake, that makes one a true minister of Jesus
Christ." [1]

He is one of the noblest defenders of liberty of
thought and faith that I have yet found in the first
half of the seventeenth century. He is always
pleading for the rights of tender conscience, and
dealt with hard old "Gangraena" Edwards as only
a high-born saint could have done: "I am afraid of
you [for you]," he says to Edwards, "Your face and
complexion shews a most sadly parched, burnt
and withered spirit. . . . Have you no gnawings,
no flashings [i. e. of conscience]? . . . I told you at
parting [they had met in the street] I hoped we
should overcome you by prayer. I believe we shall
pray you into repentance or shame or judgment
ere we are done with you." . . . "Your book of
Jeers and Stories of your brethren; poor man! It
will not long be musick in your ears at this rate of
sinning. . . . I must tell you further, that since any
of the light and glory of Christ dawned upon me;
since first I saw that morning star of Righteousness, any of the brightness of the glory in my heart,
that heart of mine that once lived in the Coasts of
Zebulun and Naphtali, in the region and shadow of
death, I can freely challenge ye, and thousands
more such as ye, to say, write, do, print anything
and I hope I shall in the strength of Christ, in
whom I am able to do all things, give you blessings
for cursings, and prayers for persecutions." [2]

[1] *Some Drops of the Viall*, p. 112.
[2] *Reasons for Unitie*. Another Seeker of the period, William

In this same tract he declares that "love is a more excellent way than ordinances. It brings peace as nothing else does. . . . That love which can love those of other kinds, as Presbyterians, Anabaptists, Independents, is not that love of a creature only: since *the more we love any that are not as we are, the lesse we love as men and the more as God.*"

He considers all external, legal, forensic stages of religious thought and practice as only steps and preparations for a religion of life and spirit. Church organizations and systems, creeds and sacraments are at best only signs and parables of an invisible Church, which the Eternal Spirit is slowly building in the hearts and lives of men. "Christ," he says, "is in all His people in spirit and truth, *as the eternal seed.*" The true Reformation, then, is not to be in Administrations, Ordinances, and Gifts, but rather to have Jesus Christ as the Eternal Seed formed in us.[1]

One of the highest points of insight that good old

Walwyn, wrote two Tracts in answer to Edwards. The first was entitled *Against the Poyson of Master Edwards* (1646). Walwyn says: "Whilst I live I trust I shall live in love and when I dye that I shall dye in this love and Rise and remain eternally in love, that is, in God (for God is love)." The other tract, *A Prediction of Mr. Edwards his Conversion and Recantation*, has this passage: "O that he (Edwards) would stand still awhile and consider the love of Christ, that he would throw by his embittered pen, lock himself close in his study, draw his curteines, and sit down but two hours and seriously, sadly and searchingly lay to heart the things he hath said and done against a people whom he knoweth desire to honour God and withal bear in mind the infinite mercies of God."

[1] *Sparkles of Glory*, pp. 189–190.

John Saltmarsh arrives at is the conviction that truth is self-evidencing when it comes to the soul, and shines by its own light within. "If there must be miracles (as some hold in order to insure belief) then Truth is not of that excellent Nature that it seems; for if it be not able to make itself evident and cast a native shine and brightness upon that soul it comes into, it is but weak, dark and in-sufficient."[1] "If," he continues, "Truth be not discernable in itself by its own glorious lightsome nature by beames from itself; it is in a worse con-dition than many things belowe, as the sun and stars and candles. . . . If there must be miracles to make us believe and not believe any Truth till then; we must have for every truth as well as for one or two, a miracle to give it evidence; and so there must be a continual and new miracle-working for every new believing. (!) . . . No miracles," he concludes, "can in their own nature make one be-lieve without a spiritual conviction from the Spirit of Christ going along with it. . . . *The only way to see Truth is to live in the power of it.*"

Here, then, was another Yorkshire "prophet" who had revolted from all existent visible Churches and forms and ceremonies, and who called upon his listeners and readers to "build all inward" and to be content with nothing less than the birth of the incorruptible seed of God in their own souls.

We must pass over now from these interpreters of the rising hope of a new dispensation of the

---

[1] *Smoak in the Temple*, p. 20.

Spirit to deal briefly with the actual Seeker communities that were formed to realize these hopes. The accounts of Seekers in Edwards, in Baxter, in Baillie, and in the other conservative defenders of the faith throw almost no light on what was actually happening, but there is sufficient information at hand of a trustworthy sort to enable us to understand this widespread revolt from all church systems, and the glowing aspiration that went with it for a pure religion of life and spirit. There were large societies of these separated people in many parts of England by the beginning of the Civil War, and they went on forming until 1652 when the Quaker movement developed and absorbed a large part of their membership. The best sources of information available are to be found in the early accounts of the rise of the Quakers, especially in the volume entitled *First Publishers of Truth*, in the Journals and other writings of early Quaker leaders who had been Seekers, and in the extensive correspondence that makes up the Swarthmore Collection of Letters. Another collection of correspondence called *Swaledale Papers* is a very illuminating source of material. The largest groups were in the Yorkshire dales and the two adjoining counties of Lancashire and Westmorland, and in other parts of Yorkshire. There were, too, bodies of Seekers in and around Bristol, and there were many individuals and groups in London committed to this way. Individuals who held Seeker views were to be found in almost all parts of the land after 1640.

George Fox himself made a complete break in 1643 with all forms of organized religion, and went out from his home on an eager quest for a religion that could "speak to his condition." His account of his state of mind, of his openings of truth, and of his experiences indicates that he belonged quite definitely in the Seeker class, though he had not yet attached himself to any existing group. In one of his earliest Tracts, *Saul's Errand to Damascus* (1653), he says: "In the north parts of Lancashire many pretious Christians have for some time past foreborne to concorporate in Parochial Assemblies, wherein they profess themselves to have gained little of the Knowledge of Jesus Christ: And it is and hath been put upon their hearts to meet often (and on the Lord's Day constantly) at convenient places to seek the Lord their Redeemer and to worship Him in Spirit and in Truth, and to speak of such things tending to mutual edification as the good Spirit of the Lord shall teach them." That is an accurate picture of what was happening in these Seeker communities in the North.

Edward Burrough, who was one of the finest of northern leaders, has given his own account of the situation in his Preface to Fox's *Great Mistery of the Great Whore* (1658). After describing his convincement as a Quaker in 1652, he speaks of "what we were before in our religious profession and practices." He says that they had originally been men of the strictest sect, by which he means intense Puritans, and of the greatest zeal in the performance of outward righteousness. "We went through and tried all sorts of teachers and ran from mountain to mountain and from man to man, and from one form to another, as many do to this day who yet remain *ungathered* to the Lord." Then he proceeds to say, after detailing the disillusionment that followed, "We ceased from the teachings of all men, and their words, and their worships, and their temples and all their baptisms and Churches, and we ceased from our own words and professions and practices in religion . . . and by the Light of Christ in us we were led out of all false ways and false preaching and false ministers and we met often together and waited upon the Lord in pure silence from our own words, all men's words, and harkened to the voice of the Lord and felt his word to burn up and beat down all that was contrary to God." [1]

That picture can be duplicated from the personal accounts of Francis Howgill, John Camm, John Audland, Isaac Penington, Mary Penington, Charles Marshall, and many others, who left the Seekers to become, in Cromwell's phrase, "happy finders."

Nothing further is needed to make the situation clear. Nearly all of them say that they began by being strict Puritans, but failed to find relief or power in their rigid performances of the letter.

[1] John Jackson in his *A Sober Word to a Serious People* (1651) says that the Seekers "come together into some place on First Days (Sundays) and at other times, as their Hearts are drawn forth and opportunity is offered." (P. 3.)

They tried one church system after another, finally
lost faith in all forms of organized Christianity and
broke away from them to "wait" and "seek" with
others of a like mind and spirit. Isaac Penington,
whose father, Sir Isaac Penington, had been an intimate friend of John Webster, says that all the
organized forms of Christianity of the period
quickly lost their "freshness and fell into deadness," and serious-minded persons kept moving on
from one to another in constant hope of finding
vitality and power, but when that hope failed they
made their bold and lonely venture as Seekers.
"It was a weary seeking and not finding," says
Mary Springett, the remarkable woman who in
1654 became Isaac Penington's wife. She had rejected all sacraments and all the forms of organized
Christianity, but she could not by her seeking find
any constructive way of life. Her pathetic testimony sounds very modern: "I knew nothing to be
so certainly of God that I could shed my blood in
the defense of it!" In this defeated state of mind
she tried to find relief in "the excesses and vani-
ties" of London society. "Yet," she wrote, "in all
this excess and folly, I would often say to myself,
what is all this to me? I do these things because I
am weary and know not what else to do. It is not
my delight, it hath no power over me. I had rather
serve the Lord, if I knew how acceptably." [1]
When she found what seemed to her to be the way
of life, she discovered that it would involve much

---

[1] *Experiences in the Life of Mary Penington.*

suffering and heavy sacrifice, for she and her husband joined the Quaker movement not far from its most dangerous crisis. But, she bravely declared, "I judged it would be well worth my utmost cost and pains to witness in myself such a change as I saw in them [the Quakers] — such power over evil human nature."

Charles Marshall belonged to the Bristol Seeker community, and his experience confirms my account. He says: "As I grew in years I grew more and more dissatisfied with lifeless empty Professions and Professors [church members]. . . . And feeling that I could not find the living among the Dead Professions [i. e. church organizations] I spent much time in retirement in the Fields and Woods." Gradually he discovered that many others were "seeking," very much as he was, and they met together and "sat down in silence, and as any found a concern on their spirits, and Inclination in their Hearts, they kneeled down and sought the Lord, so that sometimes before the day ended, there might be twenty of us might pray, men and women and sometimes children spake a few words in prayer; and we were sometimes greatly bowed and broken before the Lord in Humility and Tenderness." [1]

George Fox had passed through something very like the Seeker stage before 1652, had emerged into a profound experience of God inwardly revealed to him and had matured his message of the Light

[1] Charles Marshall, *A Short Narrative of my Pilgrimage.*

within; and it was his good fortune to give these communities of Seekers the impression that he was sent and commissioned by God to revive and restore the apostolic power and life of Christianity and to form in the world once more a living "seed" of a universal Church of the Spirit. That impression appears to have broken in on the minds of the Seeker groups without any conscious intention on the part of Fox to produce it — at least he nowhere labored to make the impression. In any case, a very large proportion of the Seeker groups, and of the individual Seekers as well, became Quakers during the years 1652–1655, and formed the central nucleus of the new movement; it is doubtful if, without this contribution of "prepared people," Fox could have builded his Society of Friends.

There was much more of this Seeker type of dissent in the American colonies than most historians of colonial life have reckoned with. It took a very stout heart to make public profession of it, since in the Puritan colonies it was certain to be met, not with a pitiless "Gangraena" response, like Edwards', but with complete ostracism, excommunication and banishment, if not something even more extreme. Consequently the attitude remained in most instances implicit and concealed rather than avowed and championed. Roger Williams is the most famous of the colonists who dared to take the perilous path of a Seeker. Anne Hutchinson was equally brave, but her type of thought falls into a different category than that of the Seeker. Williams' early difficulties with the colonial authorities did not reveal any very specific Seeker peculiarities. He showed a number of conscientious scruples which made his path thorny, but none of them clearly marks him out at this stage as belonging definitely with the Seekers. He was suspected before banishment of being contaminated with ideas of the Anabaptists, and his baptism or re-baptism by Ezekiel Holyman, the se-baptist, soon after his arrival in Providence, gives some color to that suspicion, though the influence in Providence of Richard Scott and his wife, who was Anne Hutchinson's sister, had a good deal to do with that particular act of baptistry.

What is more important is Roger Williams' next step, after his baptism. Hanbury, in *Historical Memorials*, furnishes contemporary evidence that in 1644 Williams held that "there is no Church, no sacraments, no pastors, no Church officers, no ordinances in the world, nor has been since a few years after the Apostles." Governor Winthrop in his *Diary* gives the same testimony, viz. that a few months after his baptism, Williams questioned the validity of it, "not being able to derive the authority of it from the Apostles otherwise than by the ministers of England (whom he judged to be ill authority) so he conceived God would raise up some (new) apostolic power." Cotton Mather in his *Magnalia Christi* makes the situation still more plain. Mather describes the Baptism and then says: "But Mr. Williams quickly told them, *That being himself misled, he had led them likewise out of the way*: he was now satisfied that there was none upon earth that could administer Baptism, and so that their last Baptism as well as their first, was a Nulity, for the want of *a called Administration*; he advised them therefore to forego all, to Dislike everything, and Wait for the coming of New Apostles; whereupon they dissolved themselves and became that Sort of Sect we term *Seekers*, keeping to that one Principle, That every one should have Liberty to Worship God according to the Light of his own Conscience, but owning of no Churches or Ordinances now in the World." [1]

Roger Williams' later writings, *The Bloudy Tenent*, *The Bloudy Tenent yet more Bloudy*, *Hireling Ministry none of Christs* and *George Fox Digg'd out of his Burrowes*, all show a settled Seeker position. He declares in *The Bloudy Tenent* that there is at present "no foundation for a true Church" and that the Massachusetts Puritans "have not separated from the rubbish of anti-Christian confusions and desolations" but are "worshipping God in sleepy ignorance," "by a worship wherein fellowship with God is lost." At present he sees no "begetting ministry," no "feeding and nourishing ministry," no "divine calling," no "apostolic Gifts," no persons who have "the key of David and can open." Like the English Seekers, he calls and waits for a fresh "inspiration and instigation of the

---

[1] *Magnalia Christi* (1702), Book VIII, p. 9.

Holy Spirit" and for witnesses and messengers with apostolic power.

He is as strongly set against what he calls "hireling ministry" as any English Seeker or Quaker could be. He is dead against "Divinity Degrees," "Gownes," "Childish Ceremonies," "Professional ministry" and those "pretended seed-plots and seminaries for the ministry — the Universities." He sees the Church "like a Vessel becalmed at sea, which, though it make some way by Rowing and Towing, yet nothing comparable to what it doth when the mighty gales of God's holy Spirit breathe in the wayes of His most holy Appointments." As everybody knows, Roger Williams was one of the most valiant and uncompromising advocates of complete toleration and of untrammeled right of conscience. In this, too, he was to be found in the company of the noblest of the Seekers. Roger Williams, unlike the English Seekers, failed to recognize any divine commission or apostolic power in George Fox. He attacked him with all the virility of his early fighting powers, though he was at the time an old man near the end of his days. Very little honor and no spiritual gain came to either of the combatants in this Newport-Providence controversy. The only tangible result was two rather dull and, at present, costly volumes — *George Fox Digg'd out of his Burrowes* and *A New England Fire-Brand Quenched.*

The Quaker invaders of the colonies did find, however, in Salem, in Sandwich, in Newport, in

Dover, in Long Island, around the shores of the Chesapeake and in many other places, numerous groups of Seekers who risked the dangerous adventure of joining the hated invaders and of swelling the ranks of what the early Quakers called the "seed" of the Church of the Spirit.

AN OUTBURST OF MYSTICISM OF MANY TYPES

JACOB BOEHME, in his striking *Epistles*, predicted that "the Age of the Lily" was near at hand and that its bloom would soon burst forth, especially in the cold lands of the North, where lilies are not expected. For Boehme and mystics of his line the lily is a symbol that stands for the religion of the Spirit. The nettle was the symbol for the stern dispensation of the Law. The rose was the blood-red flower that characterized the dispensation of the Son — salvation by pain and sacrifice. The coming of the lily meant in symbolic fashion the birth of the Life and Love and Joy of God in the lives of men. The Gospel in that new age was to be written in the heart of man and no longer in the letters of a Book, and "the greater things than these" which Christ promised for the dispensation of the Spirit would then become a fact. William Dell, who was one of the finest exponents of this hope in the early days of the Commonwealth era, expressed the idea in a notable sentence. "The true religion of Christ," he said, "is written in the soul and spirit of man by the Spirit of God; and the believer is the only book in which God now writes His New Testament." [1]

[1] Sermon, "Trial of Spirits," *Works*, p. 438.

It seemed for a short period to many expectant souls as though this "eternal Gospel" was about to begin in England and that the lily was at least at the budding stage. When George Fox, in a transforming moment, suddenly had the experience that "all the creation gave unto me *another smell* than before," I am convinced that consciously or unconsciously he was referring to the new smell of the lily. That experience of Fox can be dated about 1647, and the years just before and after that date, when King Charles was moving towards his doom, give us perhaps the time of greatest mystical expectancy.

Marmaduke Stephenson, who was hanged on Boston Common in 1659, left as his dying testimony a brief account of the experience which sent him out on his dangerous mission. He, too, refers not to a vision of light or to an audition, but to a fragrant smell. "In the beginning of the year 1655," Stephenson wrote from his prison just before his death, "I was at the plough in the east parts of Yorkshire in Old England near the place where my outward being [i.e. house] was, and as I walked after the plough, I was filled with the Love and the Presence of the living God which did ravish my Heart when I felt it; for it did increase and abound in me like a Living Stream, so did the Love and Life of God run through me like precious Ointment *giving a pleasant Smell*, which made me stand still."

There are certain plants of the aloe family that,

according to tradition, require a hundred years of
ripening before they burst into bloom. The generation that puts the plant into the ground and
starts it on its way toward growth has long disappeared before the blossoming time comes, and
another generation, perhaps twice removed, has the
joy of the fragrance. The ripening and bloom of
movements that affect the human spirit are still
slower and even longer delayed. The outburst of
mystical life in the mid-seventeenth century in
England, which the enthusiasts thought fore-
tokened the blossoming of the lily, had its beginnings in the great Platonic revival of the Renaissance and in the awakening of the human spirit
that came with the birth of the Reformation. The
revolt from the dominance of Aristotle and, with
that, the breaking forth afresh of the warmer and
more genial waters of the stream of Platonism, was
like the coming of the equinox after a long winter.
It has been happily said that "in every background
of the pageants of the Renaissance lurked a mystic
saint." The Plato of the Renaissance was thoroughly saturated with mystical color. It was not
the Plato of the *Dialogues* that came to them; it
was Plato seen in the light of Plotinus and Hermes
Trismegistus, the Plato of Ficino and Mirandola,
the Plato who to early Christian Fathers was the
forerunner of St. John's doctrine of the Logos, and
the original spring of all Christian mysticism.
These Platonists of the Renaissance came upon the
discovery that God is not in some remote place,

but is immanent Reason — the eternal *nous* —
present in all things, revealed wherever there is
beauty or truth or love and forever kindred to the
mind of man. This is the mystical Platonism of
Edmund Spenser's *Hymne of Heavenlie Beauty*:

Mount up aloft through heavenly contemplation,
From this dark world whose damps the soule do blynd,
And like the native brood of Eagles kynd
On that bright sunne of glory fixe thine eyes
Clear'd from grosse mists of fragile infirmities.

The stream ran on through "the ever memorable" John Hales and Jeremy Taylor. It watered
and refreshed Nicholas Ferrar of Little Giddings,
who already at six years of age was a passionate
seeker for God. It was the spring of life and beauty
in his saintly friend George Herbert. It was a
strong current in Donne and Vaughan and Cra-
shaw, and ran full flood in Thomas Traherne.
"God," declared that noble Platonist, "is ever more
near to us than we are to ourselves, so that we cannot feel our own souls without feeling Him."[1]
Traherne says that "a whispering instinct of nature" set him on a quest for God while he was still
a child.[2] Donne's great line, "All divinity is love
and wonder," packs into the briefest possible com-
pass the concentrated essence of Platonism. There
is something majestically simple in Vaughan's line,
"I saw Eternity the other night," and in Cra-
shaw's Great Lord of Love,

[1] *Centuries of Meditation*, II, 81.   [2] *Ibid.*, p. 16.

> Making his mansion in the mild
> And milky soul of a soft child.

Francis Quarles, too, belongs in the order of the Platonic mystics with his lines that had already burned like fire in his heart before he wrote them:

> I was flax and He was flames of fire:
> Our firm united souls did more than twine;
> So I my Best-beloved's am; so He is mine.

Robert Southwell, whose martyr death sealed his faith, though in fact a Roman Catholic speaks like a Quaker of the inner life:

> My conscience is my crowne,
> Contented thoughts my rest;
> *My hart is happy in it selfe,*
> *My bliss is in my breste.*

"Not where I breathe," he wrote, "but where I love, I live."

Hales, "the ever memorable" (born 1584), expressed in his beautiful English style a type of mysticism which belongs in the genuine Catholic tradition: "The Prayer which is the most forcible transcends and far exceeds all power of words [i. e. prayer of inward, quiet contemplation]. St. Paul, speaking unto us of the most effectual kind of prayer, calls it sighs and groans that cannot be expressed. . . . *It requires not the voice but the mind; not the stretching of the hands but the intention of the heart; not any outward shape or carriage of the body*

but the inward behavior of the understanding." [1]
Isaac Penington, a little later, was to say, "It is the
end of words to bring men to a knowledge of things
beyond what words can utter."

Jeremy Taylor, in words that are no less lofty
than those "golden" ones of Hales, gives a personal
description of an exalted degree of meditation
which rises to the height of wordless and imageless
meditation. "It is," he says, "the unitive way of
religion, that is, it consists in unions and adher-
ences to God; it is prayer of quietness and silence,
a meditation extraordinary, a discourse without
variety, a vision and intuition of divine excellen-
cies, an immediate entry into an orb of light and
a resolution of all our faculties into sweetness, af-
fections and staring upon divine beauty."

He proceeds in a most important passage to say
that "this experience cannot be discoursed of" but
must be "felt," and he takes the ground, which I
have long held, that continual practice of the
divine presence slowly forms in the structure of
the soul an expert capacity for apprehending God.
Note his great words: "When persons have been
long softened with the continual droppings of religion, and their spirits made more timorous [i. e.
sensitive] and apt for impression by the assiduity
of prayer and perpetual alarms of death and the
continual dying of mortification, the fancy [i. e.
creative imagination], which is a very great instrument of devotion, is continually kept warm, and in

[1] *Golden Remains* (ed. 1659), p. 153.

a disposition and aptitude to take fire and to flame out into great ascents." [1]

Sir Thomas Browne has the seed of the mystical life in this quaint passage: "Man is that true and great Amphibium, whose nature is disposed to live, not onely like other creatures in divers elements, but in divided and distinguished worlds; for though there be but one to sense, there are two [worlds] to reason, the one visible, the other invisible." [2]

Father Augustine Baker (died 1641), a Roman Catholic mystic of great range and power, and his spiritual daughter Dame Gertrude belonged to the best classical type of English mysticism, the type expounded in the *Cloud of Unknowing* — mysticism of passive, unitive contemplation, a mental state beyond words or images or thoughts. Father Baker had been an Elizabethan Protestant before his conversion to Catholicism. He had formed strong Puritan sympathies, and the Puritanic strain in him remained a vital feature of his religion throughout his life. He carried on the dark and tragic note of human life, with its depth of sin and failure occasioned by the Fall, rather than that strain of devout humanism which appears in Hales and Taylor and still more clearly in the Cambridge Platonists.

The Cambridge Platonists, or "Latitude men," as they were often called, continued throughout their lives, as William Law later did, to be loyal

---

[1] Taylor's *Life of Christ* (ed. 1850), II, 139–140.
[2] *Religio Medici*, I, 34.

members of the Church of England. There is not a taint of fanaticism about them. They showed in their lives the very flower of English culture and refinement. In fact, if one is ever to apply the word "beauty" to personal character it peculiarly fits the lives of these men; in an especial degree, I think, it fits John Smith. Their lives were "four-square," like the dimensions of the New Jerusalem. One feels in all they say and do, their breadth and depth. They have in an unusual way the quality of poise and balance. They walk their round of life amid assaults and criticisms, but through it all their spirits remain calm and unruffled. They said "yea" with great conviction, but when the rest of the world met it with a loud "nay," they quietly, without contention, went on saying "yea." Their mysticism, which was of a mild and restrained type, was not marked by rapture or emotional enthusiasm; it was rather a striking instance of an intellectual vision of God warmed and touched by intellectual love of Him.[1] Whichcote, the father of the movement, expressed their ideal in his aphorism, "The Breakings in of God upon us require a mind that is not subject to Passion, but is in a serene and quiet Posture, where there is no tumult of Imagination. . . . There is no genuine and proper effect of Religion where the mind is not composed, sedate and calm."

[1] This statement would not be quite true of Henry More in his later period when he was attracted to pseudo-mystical lines of thought and interpretation and had a fancy for occultism and hidden mysteries.

It is strange that this type of mysticism should have come to birth in the greatest nursery of Puritanism in England — Emmanuel College at Cambridge. Imagine a great mystic flowering out at Harvard in the first generation of Massachusetts Puritanism. Puritanism and mysticism were antithetical. They canceled out each other. The Puritan had once for all taken his stand on what for him was the solid rock of the Word of God. God's Word to the human race was a unique revelation of a supernatural order. It was to be found, and to be found only, in the volume of the Scriptures. No other communication from God was to be expected or admitted. The heavenly returns were all in, and all spiritual truth for the ages was deposited there in that Book. The Puritan, therefore, had no expectation that any divine word was likely to break in over his threshold. The soul for him was not oracular. He was no less intense than the greatest mystic was. His physical frame trembled with awe and reverence; but he knew of no shekinah within himself where he could meet and commune with the Eternal. The shekinah was in the Ark of the Covenant.

John Bunyan is a striking case in point. He possessed all the psychological traits of a mystical disposition. His autobiographical story would incline a reader to look for mystical experiences to occur in him. He shows structural lines and tendencies very similar to those in young George Fox. With a slight change of inward climate he would

have experienced a mystical pilgrimage. Bunyan
heard voices and had "incursions" like his contemporary. One of these two men developed into a
mystic and the other did not. The essential point
of difference was in the fact of mental climate and
expectation. Bunyan's entire stock of religious
ideas was in harmony with the Puritan system of
thought, while Fox from some source had drawn
upon the well-known mental climate of the spiritual reformers and the Seekers. He expected something new to break into his soul from God, while
Bunyan could not dream of a genuine communication given him from any higher source than Satan,
to whom he assigned his "voices" and "incursions."

It makes one wonder, therefore, how a signal
mystical movement could come to birth in the
Puritan atmosphere of Emmanuel College.[1] The
fact is that Benjamin Whichcote, the leader of the
movement, though thoroughly familiar with all the
orthodox lines of faith from Calvin and Beza and
Knox, really formed his inward life on a wholly
different line of spiritual culture. Bishop Burnet,
who knew the facts well, says that Whichcote

[1] The persons who are included in this famous group are: Benjamin Whichcote (1609–83), John Smith (1618–52), Ralph Cudworth
(1617–88), John Norris of Bemerton (1657–1711), Nathaniel Culver-
well (1618?–51), Henry More (1614–87), Peter Sterry (died 1672)
and closely affiliated with them, especially with More, Francis Mer-
cury van Helmont, Lady Anne Conway of Ragley Hall and George
Keith, all three of whom were for a period members of the Society of
Friends.

studied Plato and Tully and Plotinus, bent on discovering "a seed of deiform nature" in man. He
was, too, profoundly influenced by the teaching of
those noble forerunners William Chillingsworth,
John Hales, and Jeremy Taylor. I cannot prove it,
but I am confident that John Everard's sermons
and, even more, his translations of the spiritual
reformers and mystics were, as well, notable influences in the formation of Whichcote's mind and
in the shaping of his "expectation."

Whichcote came to believe in his early manhood
that there is "a seed of God," "a seminal principle," "something that comes immediately from
God," in the fundamental nature of man's inmost
being. "God," he said in one of his sermons, "is
more inward to us than our own souls are. . . .
Were it not for God we should not know the
Powers of our souls which have an appropriation
to God." [1] Again he declares that "When we make
nearer approaches to God, we have more use of
ourselves," [2] i. e. we are completer selves.

If we are to call this type of religion mysticism,
the word must be used to mean that reason in man
has a godlike capacity to apprehend its great
Original, to attain a vision of God and to come into
conformity with Him whose we are and whom we
serve. In short, in the words of Whichcote's favorite text, "the spirit of man is a candle of the Lord,"
i. e. man at his best is essentially a revealing place
for God. Holiness, as Whichcote insists, belongs

---

[1] *Aphorism*, p. 861.   [2] *Ibid.*, p. 709.

to man's right constitution and temper — it is the coming of complete health and strength.[1]

John Norris of Bemerton was a deep and quiet soul, withdrawn from the din of the world and in tune with the harmonies of the eternal world within the visible one. He held an exalted view of the native grandeur of man's reason, and took it for granted that the soul by contemplation can return to the supreme good from which it has come:

> See to what new region am I come.
> I know it well, it is my native home.

"The soul of man is the native country and region of Truth," since God is the place of spirits as space is the place of bodies. We partake of Truth because as rational beings we partake of Him. But beyond that, there is a moral union through love which brings immediate contact with God and a central touch.[2]

Henry More, even in his childhood, had "an inward sense of the divine presence." When he was fifteen years old, the reality of God overtopped in his mind any other reality, though this was followed by a loop of darkness and doubt, from which he finally emerged into "a most joyous and lucid state of mind." He was at this time "solicitous about nothing so much as a more full union with the divine and celestial Principle, the inward well-spring of life eternal." He became convinced that

[1] *Several Discourses*, IV, 92.
[2] *Theory of the Ideal World*, and addresses on "Reason and Faith."

man's soul is "a precious drop sunk from Aeternitie." Out of his own experiences and studies came forth in 1660 his greatest book, *The Grand Mystery of Godliness*, which according to the testimony of a prominent book-seller of the day, "ruled all book-sellers in London for twenty years." More, in spite of his early fierce opposition to popular forms of mysticism, in movements such as Familism and Quakerism, was himself continually interpreting the inward Light as a central principle of religion, and it was directly due to him, though not by his intention, that George Keith became a Quaker.

Peter Sterry is the only other member of this group to whom I can now refer. He graduated B.A. at Emmanuel College the same year that Whichcote proceeded M.A. (1633). He was elected a Fellow in 1636 and received his M.A. in 1637. None of the Emmanuel College men of the time were more thoroughly grounded in Platonism than was Sterry, and his Platonism included an intimate acquaintance with Plotinus, Proclus, Dionysius the Areopagite and Ficino. He was more temperamentally and fundamentally a mystic — a born mystic — than any other member of this Cambridge group. His writings include a sermon on *The Spirit's Conviction of Sinne* (1645), *The Clouds in which Christ Comes* (1648), and three books published posthumously, viz. *A Discourse of Freedom of the Will* (1675), *The Rise, Race and Royalty of the Kingdom of God in the Soul of Man* (1683), and *The Appearance of God to Man in the Gospel* (1710). He was a friend of Henry Vane, who shared his mystical interests, which gave Baxter the opportunity for his pun, "Vanity and Sterility were never more happily conjoined." Sterry was voted preacher to the Council of State after the execution of Charles I, and was later given lodgings at Whitehall, where he usually preached both Sundays and mid-week before Cromwell, who was in full sympathy with the mystical strain that dominated Sterry's sermons. Lord Rosebery surprised his readers by calling Cromwell "a practical mystic," but he might truthfully have made Cromwell's mysticism even more emphatic than he did. Remembering the great text which he learned at Emmanuel College, "The spirit of man is a candle of the Lord," Sterry finely says, "When one candle is lighted, we light many by it, and when God hath kindled the Life of His Glory in one man's Heart he often enkindles many by the flame of that." [1] The steadily growing sympathy which Cromwell showed in his later period with mystics and Seekers was in no small measure due to the kindling influence of Sterry's beautiful spirit. Legal religion Sterry compared to "a spark struck from flint at midnight," while the religion of the Spirit, he said, is "a living, gushing, perpetual Fountain."

Carlyle, commenting on George Fox's first visit to Cromwell and their talk together about "the Unfathomable Universe and the Light in it from

[1] *Rise, Race and Royalty*, p. 39.

above and the Darkness in it from below," says significantly, "Yes, George, this Protector has a sympathy with the Perennial; and feels it across the Temporary: no hulls, leathern or other, can entirely hide it from the sense of him." [1] There can be no doubt, I think, that this strange man of destiny, who was as mysterious to himself as he was to his own generation, and as he still remains to all who have endeavored to understand him, "felt the Perennial, the Eternal, in the midst of the Temporary," and that is, perhaps, as good a definition as we are likely to get of mysticism.

In the debates in the Army, which are reported in the *Clarke Papers*, Cromwell said with deep feeling, "I am one of those whose heart God hath drawn out to wait for some extraordinary dispensations according to those promises He hath set forth of things to be accomplished in the latter time and I cannot but think that God is beginning of them." [2] It sounds, no doubt, more like a Seeker than a mystic, but it is a notable point that Cromwell felt convinced that the new dispensation of the Spirit had begun already in the "hearts of those whom God hath drawn out," of whom he was one. Writing to his daughter Bridget in 1646 of the spiritual state of his other daughter, Lady Claypole, Cromwell said, "She seeks after what will satisfy. And thus to be a Seeker is to be of the best sect next to a finder, and such shall every faithful,

[1] *Oliver Cromwell* (Century edition), III, 225.
[2] *Clarke Papers*, I, 379.

humble seeker be at the end. Happy seeker, happy finder!"

This noble stream of spiritual religion — at least semi-mystical in character — which flowed through the "Latitude men" of Emmanuel College watered the lives of a multitude of unnamed persons as well as of some who were the makers of history. It flowed on through William Law a century later, and broke out still another century later in fertilizing power in the life and writings of Samuel Taylor Coleridge.[1]

Some of the writings of the Cambridge Platonists, at quite an early period, were within reach of the New England Puritans, and may have been read by an occasional liberal, though there is little evidence that they colored the stream of thought. Plato's complete *opera*, with some of the works of Porphyry, Iamblicus, and Hermes Trismegistus, were early put into the Harvard Library. Plotinus and Ficino were there in Latin. Theophilus Gale, who is often included among the Cambridge Platonists, presented his own works to the College Library, and they were certainly read by both Increase and Cotton Mather, and by some other Puritan divines. In the eighteenth century both Harvard and Yale had long lists of the books of the leading Cambridge Platonists on their shelves. But no important Puritan mystic appears before Jonathan Edwards.

[1] Coleridge quotes John Smith with admiration in his *Aids to Reflection* and in his *Literary Remains*, and he was close to these men in religious thought.

We must pass over now from the mystical religion of refined scholars and Platonists to consider the mysticism of the common man — often crude and uncouth as well as plain and uncultured. We shall find it expressed, too, for the most part no longer through individual persons but rather through social groups, fused together by a common experience into small spiritual fellowships, or "beloved communities."

We shall in this section be dealing with a new stage of mystical life and thought and interpretation, so different from classical mysticism that it is with difficulty covered by the same word. And yet there is no better word at hand than mysticism to express the central aspect of this stage of religious life. The focal idea in this new type of mysticism is the glowing faith that there is something divine in man, which under right influences and responses can become the dominant feature of a person's whole life. The favorite text of the exponents of this affirmation mysticism was that noble oracular fragment in Proverbs already quoted: "The spirit of man is a candle of the Lord." This line of thought goes back for its pedigree, without much doubt, to the humanism of the Renaissance. Humanism is a looser word even than mysticism, and its many revivals and reappearances have taken on many varied types of meaning. The humanism which profoundly influenced the Reformation period was at heart deeply Neoplatonic and mystical. It reinterpreted man as a divine-

human being, that is to say, as man plus a Beyond
akin to himself. The Over-Soul or Over-Mind aspect of life, later brought forward vividly by Emer-
son, was of course not formulated in the sixteenth
century, but it was implicitly held wherever Neo-
platonic humanism flourished. It was taken for
granted in all the circles of these mystical groups
that emerged out of this humanist movement that
man is over-individual inwardly in relation to God.
The new mysticism, like the old, made much of
withdrawal from the strain and stress of life. It
emphasized the need of hush and quiet. Concen-
tration, contemplation, recollection, were as much
stressed in the affirmation type as they had ever
been in the negation or classical type of mysticism.
If man's tiny, fragmentary self is to complete itself,
through correspondence with God's indwelling and
surrounding Life, then a person must cease to focus
on "things" and must open from within the win-
dows and doors of his soul for the More than himself to come in and enlarge and consecrate him.
Hans Denck finely expressed the divine-human relationship of life when he said, in words which
anticipated Pascal, "Apart from God no one can
seek or find God, for he who seeks God in very
truth already has Him." Thomas Traherne, who
is a unique interpreter of this affirmation point of
view, wrote in his *Centuries of Meditation*, "You
are never your true self till you live by your soul
more than by your body, and you never live by
your soul until you feel its incomparable excel-

lence," by which he means that the soul is "a centre
of Eternity." The idea is expressed as well as it
can be in the lines

> I know not what my secret is;
> I know but it is mine:
> I know to live for it were bliss,
> To die for it divine.

The earliest of these mystical communities to be
formed in England was the "Family of Love," or
the "Familists," as they were usually called. The
propaganda accounts written by heresy hunters
against this sect furnish no basis of historical reality at all, and may be entirely discounted. The
terms "horrible sect," "monstrous heresy," "foule
and filthy errours," which are flung against them
are imaginative creations of minds that could admit only one form of true religion. "Fanatics"
there were no doubt in the Family of Love, as
there are in all movements that are intense, and
immoral persons certainly did sometimes attach
themselves to it for reasons of self-interest, but for
the most part Familism was a clean, pure type of
life. It was at heart a revolt from form and letter
and a serious attempt on the part of honest people
to eradicate sin from human nature and to become
united with God in life and truth and love.

The Family, or House of Love, was founded by a
remarkable mystic, named Henry Nicholas (or
Niclaes), who was born in Münster in Westphalia

about 1501.[1] He was a religious phenomenon as a
boy, living retired and apart from other children,
puzzling his head over problems of faith instead of
playing games, and arriving at spiritual insights
far beyond his years. From the first, even when he
was only eight, he insisted that religion was futile
unless it produced a state of godliness and righteousness of life and brought about the destruction
of sin in man. From his ninth year he began to
have visions and openings and he felt himself
powerfully "invaded" by the divine Spirit and
raised to what he later called "a begodded person." He married happily and succeeded in mer-
cantile business, but always felt convinced that
through him God intended to "reveal His perfect
Truth on earth." He removed to Amsterdam about
1530, and later to Emden, and during a somewhat
lengthy period of disappearance and concealment
he was perhaps in England. He pored over the
Bible and brooded over the meaning of life and
salvation. He studied the writings of Luther, but
disapproved of his basis of reformation. He was
subject to trance and ecstasy, and in a memorable experience felt himself enwrapt by God and
raised into union with Him in true mystical fashion; in this state he believed that he was chosen to

[1] There are three unpublished manuscripts in the Maatschappy
Library in Leyden which contain the main sources for the life and
experiences of Nicholas. Dr. F. Nippold, in *Zeitschrift für die his-
torische Theologie* (Jahrgang 1862, Heft III), has admirably interpreted Nicholas and his movement, drawing his material mainly from
these manuscripts.

be the revealer both of the Divine Nature and of the spiritual possibilities of man. From that time on his initials H. N. stand in his mind for *homo novus* — the new man, the new Adam — through whom the Light of God was to break for the new age of the world. The symbol used frequently in his books was a heart and a blooming plant with three branches, — almost certainly the lily, — and the letters L. W., which were the initials in Dutch for Liefde and Waarheid (love and truth). The heart bears as its superscription the letters H. N.

It is impossible to follow the details of Nicholas' life or the history of his movement on the Continent. He was plainly enough a psychopathic person, and was possessed of exalted notions, as the founders of religions are apt to be, but withal he attained an extraordinary quality of human love, an absence of wrangling, bluster, and violence, and a spirit of peace and gentleness. He was a voluminous writer, and his religious movement spread in England largely through the translation and circulation of his books. There were no less than twenty-three volumes in succession, of which *Spiegel der Gerechtigkeit* (*The Glass of Righteousness*) was considered to be his most important one.[1] *An Introduction to the Glass of Righteousness* presents an interpretation of his central ideas. His *Evangelium Regni* is a serious call to an inward

[1] This book has never been translated into English and is extremely rare. It is significant that George Fox owned one of the few copies.

type of Christianity, and his *Spiritual Land of Peace* is a kind of Pilgrim's Progress of the soul of man.

The Family of Love began to spread in England about 1575, though it probably had English converts even before that date, and it eventually became exclusively an English movement, slowly vanishing on the Continent. The most successful early propagator of it was a Dutch joiner named Christopher Vitells, who was "a great spreader of the sect" in the Diocese of Ely, and in Cambridge-shire in general. Vitells was the first translator of Nicholas. The "fraternity" was composed of weavers, basket-makers, musicians, bottle-makers, and other laborers who traveled at their trades and so disseminated their faith and their way of life. All the available sources of information, both friendly and hostile, indicate a rapid growth of the movement and a steady progress of its principles, especially among the common people, though they occasionally found here and there a scholar who would help to translate the books of H. N. for them. By the beginning of the Commonwealth era Familists were numerous in London and the counties, and the leaven had spread into the colonies. The name "Familists" was loosely used, especially by strict Churchmen, as an opprobrious term for any disliked sectary. Grindletonians and Seekers were often called Familists, as we have seen, which only implied that they were a "bad lot," with radical traits and proclivities.

The Familists of the Commonwealth era may be briefly characterized as follows: In many respects they were like Seekers, so that those who confused the two sects were not wholly to blame. They found all existing Churches inadequate and spiritually bankrupt. They forsook the safe way of conformity because it seemed to them to end in inward poverty. H. N., in his *Evangelium Regni*, says that "many goodwilling Hearts with anguish of mind, have diligently sought for the Light and the Truth and have wondered whether they were anywhere to be found, or whether they might once more break forth." The main criticism which the Familists made of the churches was on account of their spiritual sterility and deadness. They looked for the fruits of the Spirit in these churches and found only dry rustling leaves. They complained that the churches did not look for transformation in their members, that they even pleaded for sin and failure in Christians and expected them to say that they were "miserable sinners," as though nothing better were possible for poor weak human nature. It seemed to them that the churches all lacked expectancy. They were threshing over the old straw of controversy and debate. The miracle of the new life, raised out of death and sin to a triumphant quality, appeared to be everywhere wanting.

The Familist, on the other hand, stood unflinchingly for holiness of life and for the perfection of human nature here on earth. They were extremely opposed to all manner of *forensic religions* that offered man a vision of relief on the ground that Christ had "done enough for us" to ensure salvation. For them there is no salvation possible for man until he himself dies completely to sin and the love of it, becomes born of the Spirit, and is raised in resurrection power to a new life. Not only must H. N. be a *homo novus*, but every person who is worthy to be called a Christian must become a new Adam, through whom God's nature becomes "manned" as in Christ He took on perfectly our nature, and "this new man" must be "godded with God" in the spirit of perfect Love.

Nobody has ever expected more of man's possibilities than did the Familists, in fact they stretched their "expectation" almost to the breaking point. Their opponents called them Arians, but they were not properly speaking Arian Unitarians. They did not level Christ down to mere human nature. What they did do was to raise human nature in its potential capacity to the level of the highest divinity. They took St. Paul literally when he said that men must "grow up into Him who is the Head," and "attain unto a full-grown man, unto the measure of the stature of the fulness of Christ" so that "He might be the first born among many brethren." That there are dangers involved in such a magnificent hope can hardly be doubted, but that perilous path the Familists took.

The lofty attainment which was their goal was not, however, to be reached by a slow ethical upward pull, in their own strength. It was for them essentially a mystical event. As soon as man became "goodwilling" and so completely "ready" for the event, God, by His Spirit, would, they believed, raise human nature to its divine possibilities and make the person of that type a "godded man," as at first in Adam he had been. The "community of love," as they called their little communities of believers, practised corporate silence and group worship, made much of "expectancy," dwelt upon the divine possibilities of man and thus produced an intense mystical climate for each aspiring member to share and to live in. It worked effectively with certain types of persons, but it obviously could not be made a universal faith.

One of its greatest weaknesses was its top-heavy system of organization. It did not share with the contemporary religious movements of the period their democratic basis of government. It had an elaborate order of priesthood, with "a highest Bishop," "twenty four Elders," then "the Seraphim or Archbishops." Below that triple order there were in addition three other lower orders of priests. The process of consecration and ordination for all these orders was extremely elaborate and complicated. Then there were sacraments to be practised, which though only symbolic in character were raised to a pitch of great importance for the members of the Family. All this extensive external system fitted in badly with the mystical aspects of the movement. It turned many away who were otherwise attracted by the mystical feature of the society. What happened in the end was that the movement broke down and failed in its organized character, while the central ideas and ideals of it attained a great vogue. The translations of Nicholas' books had a large circle of readers, and each took what he liked and left the rest. These little books were consequently the spreaders of a wave of mystical thought and aspiration, with no corresponding body or system to give it form and unity. Before Jacob Boehme's writings were translated into English the Family of Love was the most important source of popular mysticism in England.

I am convinced that this was the source of Anne Hutchinson's views, which so powerfully disturbed the peace of Boston and Cambridge three hundred years ago. Modern writers have complained, as did John Winthrop, that they were "a theological jargon which no man understood." It does not seem that way to me at all. The moment the fierce controversy is read in the light of its historical background it becomes quite lucid. Anne Hutchinson, and still more clearly her brother-in-law, the Rev. John Wheelwright, who was banished from the Colony before she was, sharply differentiated two types of religion: "the covenant of works" and "the covenant of Grace." These terms were in the air in England at the time. The former stood for "legal religion" — what I have called *forensic religion*. It was based on written commands and promises, external happenings and conformity to

sacred systems which were considered to be effica-
cious in their own right. To Anne Hutchinson that
was all "elementish"; it was only a disciplinary
stage, and she soundly scored the ministers who
were still living in it and preaching it.

The "covenant of Grace," on the other hand,
was the full-grown stage of spiritual religion in
which, to quote Winthrop once more, "the true
Christian becomes united with the holy Spirit and
hath no longer merely gifts and graces, but hath
the holy Spirit Himself." Winthrop says that
Wheelwright claimed that "the Person of the Holy
Ghost and a believer were united." Hugh Peters
of Salem bore his testimony that Mrs. Hutchinson
"spoke out plump that we ministers were not
sealed, that we preached in judgment [i.e. theory]
but not in *experience*." The whole controversy
turns on that pivot, whether religion is to consist of
first-hand experience, tested in heart and life and
action, or whether it is to be a forensic theory,
argued from texts and defended by texts. Mrs.
Hutchinson's "heresy" consisted in the claim that
her religion was by "immediate revelation,"
mystical experience, and inward certainty. She
was, perhaps, not a full-fledged Familist, but she
was assuredly talking in the patois of H. N.'s little
books.

Lady Deborah Moody and her friends, who mi-
grated from Lynn to Gravesend on Long Island,
were more impregnated with the ideas of the Anabaptists than Anne Hutchinson appears to have

been in her Boston period, but there seems to have
been a strong mystical strain as well in that curious
group of spiritual "expecters." Samuel Gorton of
Warwick, Rhode Island, was not over-well balanced, but he, too, in his mystical groping appears
to have belonged at least on the left wing of the
Family of Love.

Throughout the entire period of this outburst of
mystical fervor there was always a left-wing fringe
to the movements which came close to the perilous
edge of safety and sanity. The word "Ranter"
was coined to characterize those who made up this
fringe. The Ranters were, in my judgment, not a
specific sect of people. They formed the rather
wild tag-end of the various intense religious movements of the time. There were Ranters in almost
all the sects. There were some plain lunatics
among them; there were many persons who were
loaded with complexes, and still more who were in
unstable equilibrium and had pushed the pantheistical tendencies of the period to dangerous extremes. Persons of this type drew kindred spirits
around them by a kind of hypnotic spell or contagion of ideas, and thus half-mad groups were
formed at many places very much like the bands
of "the Brethren of the Free Spirit" in the thirteenth century. Their half-digested ideas of "the
Allness of the All" made them ready to claim that
any inclination or impulse or sudden thought was a
revelation of the will of God. They completely discounted outward helps, tests, and standards, and

pushed inward light and immediate inspiration beyond all known limits. In some respects this surge of subjectivism was a valuable lesson to the contemporary leaders of mystical movements, especially to the Quakers, for it drove vigorously home to their consciousness the dangers that beset any such over-emphasis of the inward that the test and balance of the external factors are lost and the cumulative gains of history neglected. Jacob Bauthumley stated the Ranter's creed in a way that would make a serious person stop and meditate. "It is not so safe," he said, "to go to the Bible to see what others have spoken and writ of the mind of God as to see what God speaks within me and to follow the doctrine and leadings of it in me." [1]

George Fox frequently dwells upon "the high imaginations" in which the Ranters indulged, with no power to discern right from wrong or good from bad or truth from error. But who is to decide between what is "high imagination" stuff and what is "heavenly vision"? I have a recurrent dream in which I climb an immense mountain peak that towers over all other mountain peaks in its range. Sometimes I go up with a guide and sometimes alone, but always from the top I see over the world and gaze out on a scene of marvelous beauty and have that feeling of exaltation which all mountain climbers know, when I have mastered all the difficulties and have conquered my peak. But, alas,

[1] *The Light and Dark Sides of God* (London, 1650), p. 77.

in a few minutes I come awake and find myself
flat in bed and a thousand miles from any peak.
The whole thing was "high imagination." The
Ranter shakes us awake, whether he gets his own
eyes open or not, and makes us realize that if we are
going to get anywhere with mysticism we must
learn how to distinguish between will-o'-the-wisp
flashes and solid illuminative contributions to the
spiritual wealth of the world.

One of the most massive streams of mystical influence that poured from the outside into the confused life and thought of England during the
Commonwealth era came from the writings of
Jacob Boehme, the Silesian Protestant mystic, who
died in 1624. His extensive works were all put into
English between the years 1647 and 1661, through
the diligent efforts of John Sparrow, John Ellistone,
and Henry Blunden. The story of his life and some
parts of his writings had been passed about in
manuscript before 1647, when his first book to be
translated into English, the *Forty Questions*, was
printed. The response to these books was immediate and profound.

There were three characteristic strands of
thought in Boehme. One was a more or less occult
strand drawn from current alchemy. It tends to
spoil Boehme for the modern reader, but it only
added to his fascination for a large body of readers
in the seventeenth century. His most important
contribution, as I view him, was his powerful interpretation of a vital type of salvation as contrasted

with the forensic systems that had emerged from the Reformation. No one has succeeded better in driving home the fact that salvation is a fictitious claim until the man himself is delivered from the love of sin and is raised into a new moral and spiritual power and walks in newness of life. This note in Boehme appealed powerfully to the Seekers, to the Familists, and to Henry More and other Cambridge Platonists, as it did later to William Law.

Finally Boehme was, in an extraordinarily profound sense, a mystic — a man whose whole being was penetrated and fused with the conviction that he had come into living personal relations with God. There was, too, valid ground for thinking that what had come to him was "real experience" and not "high imagination," for his life was thoroughly transformed by it, raised to new spiritual levels, endued with rare qualities of wisdom and insight, and withal made able to endure persistent persecution and abuse with the gentleness and sweetness of a hundred-horse-power saint. It was probably the mystic aspect in Boehme that most deeply influenced seventeenth-century England. He became the father of a special sect called the "Behmenites," but much more important than that was his far-reaching mystical influence on spiritually-minded individuals, like Justice Durant Hotham, and on the better class of members in the various sectarian groups. He had prophesied that the lily would bloom in the North, and he probably

did more than any one before George Fox to further the blossoming of that particular lily in
England.

All these streams of mystical life converged in the
Quaker movement, which, beginning very feebly in
1647, spread extensively and rapidly after 1652,
and accumulated in the face of stubborn persecution not far from a hundred thousand members at
home and abroad before the death of Fox in 1691.
The influence of the Cambridge Platonists on the
Quakers is least in evidence of all these mystical
groups, and one can only wish that its contact had
been more marked. Only Henry More of the entire fellowship of Latitude men had any effective
place with the Quaker leaders, and even he made
no impression on Fox. He strongly influenced
Keith and Lady Conway, and had some good
contacts with Barclay, Penn, Penington, George
Whitehead, and John Whitehead, but except in the
case of Keith he had no shaping influence of any
note.

The contribution from the Familists was probably greater than that from any of the other sectaries, except the Seekers, who have already been
dealt with. The early part of Fox's *Journal* reveals
a strong Familist strain in him. He had no sympathy with their form of organization or with their
sacraments, but he was plainly impressed with
their religious experiences and ideas, especially
with their emphasis on the transformation of life
and on the attainment of perfection here on earth.

In Mansfield, at the beginning of his mission, he cried out, "Do ye not see the blood of Christ? See it in your hearts, to sprinkle your hearts and consciences from dead works to serve the living God; ... for," he continues, "I saw the blood of the New Covenant [i. e. "the Covenant of Grace"] how it came into the heart." The blood of Christ is, for him, no longer legal and forensic; it is an operative power in his own inmost being. Among some people of high profession in Leicestershire, Fox asked "whether their mountain of sin was brought down and laid low in them and their rough and crooked ways made smooth and straight *in them*" — "for they looked upon the Scriptures as meaning outward mountains and ways. But I told them *they must find these things in their own hearts*." At Derby he told his listeners that "all their preaching, baptism and sacrifices would never sanctify them, and I bade them look unto Christ [formed] within them. . . . At last they asked me whether I was sanctified. I answered 'Yes; for I am in the Paradise of God.' Then they asked me if I had no sin. I answered 'Christ my Saviour has taken away my sin, and in Him is no sin.' They asked me how we knew Christ did abide in us. I said 'By His Spirit that He hath given us.' They temptingly asked if any of us were Christ. I answered 'Nay, we are nothing, Christ is all.' They said, 'If a man steal, is it no sin?' I answered, 'All unrighteousness is sin.'" In Manchester, where he "declared truth," he says that the professors (i.e. Church members) "were in a rage," "all pleading for sin and imperfection, and could not endure to hear talk of perfection, and of a holy and sinless life." The most exalted of his claims was the one that he was "renewed into the image of God by Christ Jesus, to the state of Adam (*homo novus*) which he was in before he fell. . . . I was immediately taken up in spirit to see into another or more steadfast state than Adam's innocency, even into a state in Christ Jesus that should never fall."

Fox implied throughout his early period that a man can become "godded" with the Christ-life and be raised above sin and the love of it, and he vigorously scored Christian "professors" who expected to continue on forever as "miserable sinners." The evidence is convincing, too, that many Familists became Friends, and that the earlier movement gradually went over into and was absorbed by the new one.

The *Journal* reveals that Fox's contacts with the Ranters were frequent and important. Their mystical passion attracted him; their loose morality revolted him. He had no sympathy with their misty pantheism, though on one occasion he accepted a pipe of tobacco from a Ranter and smoked it, lest the Ranter should think, as Fox puts it, that "I did not have unity with the creation," i. e. did not admit that tobacco was a part of God's world. The Ranter influence was, in the main, negative and corrective. Many Ranters became Friends, and there was a small left-wing fringe in the early Society. But steadily Fox and his wiser associates learned wisdom from the dangers that came to light in the high claims and glowing imaginations of the Ranter element; and the new Society, while remaining no less mystical, grew all the time more balanced, and developed group tests and objective standards to try and prove and verify the inward light of the individual.

James Nayler, who in power of leadership and in his gift as a convincing preacher came close after Fox, passed through a short period of mental fog and aberration during which he was influenced by a Ranter element and was caught in the swirl of this powerful vortex. The suffering which was meted out to him as penalty for the misguided course he took was terrible in its brutality, but it brought him back to sanity and serenity. And out of his deepened life came one of the most beautiful dying testimonies of that century. It is as follows: "There is a spirit which I feel, that delights to do no evil, nor to revenge any wrong, but delights to endure all things, in hope to enjoy its own in the end: its hope is to outlive all wrath and contention, and to weary out all exaltation and cruelty, or whatever is of a nature contrary to itself. It sees to the end of all temptations. As it bears no evil in itself, so it conceives none in thought to any other. If it be betrayed it bears it; for its ground and spring is the mercies and forgiveness of God. Its crown is meekness, its life is everlasting love unfeigned; it takes its kingdom with entreaty, and not with contention, and keeps it by lowliness of mind. In God alone it can rejoice, though none else regard it, or can own its life. It is conceived in sorrow and brought forth without any to pity it; nor does it murmur at grief and oppression. It never rejoiceth but through sufferings; for with the world's joy it is murdered. I found it alone, being forsaken; I have fellowship therein with them who lived in dens and desolate places in the earth, who through death obtained this resurrection and eternal holy life."

Boehme's influence is certainly apparent in Fox's *Journal*, but it is not so certain that the Silesian mystic had much formative influence on his life and development as a young Seeker. They were very much alike in their experiences, they had many points of similarity, they both ran true to the main current of the spiritual reformers, but it is quite likely that Fox had pretty much found his trail before he was consciously aware of the light of Boehme's torch. The Quaker movement, nevertheless, does in large measure fulfil the aspirations and the yearnings of this striking man, who died the year Fox was born.

It may be taken for granted, I think, that Fox was unaware of his immense debt to the contemporary movements and spiritual interpreters. The ideas and central truths which burst into his consciousness as "openings," "insights," and "incursions" were in the air. They were in books and were being preached in closets, if not from house tops, but they were not real to Fox, and did not move him to action until they surged up *in him* and were born of his flesh and blood. He was profoundly mystic in his build and nurture, and he found his way forward mainly from within. He did not originate the ideas which his movement incarnated, but he personally discovered them, identified himself with them, poured his life through them, and with his integrated and kindled personality became the organizer of a new type of mystical society that was admirably fitted to be the carrier and distributer of this accumulated stock of spiritual truth and to be the quickening stimulus to mystical experience in others, generation after generation.

V

THE "COMMON MAN" COMES BACK

THE attempts which the "common man" made to reform the Church root and branch in the sixteenth century went awry. The failure was due to many causes: to lack of insight and judgment on the part of the leaders, to the immense complication of the task in hand, to the fact that there had not yet been historical steps of preparation taken for such a momentous undertaking, and, finally, to the fact that all the conservative powers and interests of society combined forthwith to defeat and submerge the attempts. But "lost causes" are seldom actually lost if they aim at goals of life that permanently enrich the race, and if they conform to potential aptitudes and capacities in human nature and human society.

We have seen in the preceding chapters how these movements that were submerged on the Continent rose again to life long afterwards in England and had a new day, with unexpected results and expansions. The Anabaptists always intended to reconstruct the social order and rebuild the world as well as to reform the Church. And, by one of the unexpected turns of history, the democratic principle of church organization, which the Anabaptists were the first in modern times to put in practice, and which had a rebirth in the sects which I have been reviewing, widened out, enlarged its scope and, through numerous experiments, became in the course of time the basic principle of English and American government. It is difficult if not impossible for us to realize with any degree of vividness the immense expansion of life and freedom that has come to the world through these religious efforts of the common man.

It was the suspicion of the possibility of revolutionary changes that aroused widespread terror in Europe when the movement first emerged. It was easy to foresee that if the common man could succeed in managing his church for himself, he might leap to the perverse conclusion that he could manage the State as well. The birth of the Brownist self-governing church near the end of Elizabeth's reign, and still more the expanded movement under Barrowe and Greenwood, produced a similar fear in the heart of the English officials. The intimations that lay hid in autonomous church government were seen by the watchful authorities from the very first. The powerful emphasis of the Reformation on individualism and the right of private conscience was one of the aspects that most disturbed the guardians of the old order. With a sure instinct for self-preservation they scented at once the dangers that lurked in that note of personal freedom. Luther's challenging message in his early document, *The Liberty of a*

Christian Man, carried implications which those who ran might easily read.

The leaders of the Reformation themselves saw the explosive character of the ideas with which their message was charged, and they moved over, often unconsciously, to the side of the conservative forces. Inconsistency is written large in the works of all the reformers, not the least so in the *Institutes* of Calvin. There were always two sides of the shield to be read. Romans 13:1, "Let every soul be in subjection to the higher powers," etc., was a favorite text of the leaders in their conservative moments. They endeavored in this way to insulate the live wires that carried their dangerous currents.

But even Calvin himself, the most aristocratic in temperament of all the reformers, occasionally in his sermons and more than once in his *Institutes* spoke out in favor of active resistance on conscientious grounds against "wicked and tyrannous" rulers. A ruler who "deceitfully betrays the liberty of the people over whom he has been appointed the protector by the ordinance of God" was admitted by Calvin no longer to deserve to have St. Paul's text applied to him. John Knox and Thomas Cartwright found aid and comfort for their political struggles in these cautious concessions of Calvin. Beza was far more bold and outspoken on the side of resistance and of the people's inherent rights. The treatise entitled *Du Droit des Magistrats*, published anonymously about 1573 and generally ascribed to Beza, positively claims that the people of a country have the right of redress when rulers are unfaithful to their trust, and the writer then announces a quite advanced doctrine of popular sovereignty, though he fails to make clear how the people are to assert and achieve their rights.

The Puritans showed the same caution and similar inconsistencies to those found in the writings of the reformers. They were prone to quote the *Epistle to the Romans*, and they granted that rulers were chosen by God's decrees to be the ministers of His inscrutable purposes. But they assumed that the rulers who had the benefit of St. Paul's text were those ruling on the side of truth and righteousness. Rulers of the opposite type always found the Puritans stern persons to deal with.

They always presented revolutionary aspects that seemed menacing to the representatives of the old order. There was a bold, uncompromising attitude native to the Puritan mind. Queen Elizabeth expressed her fears of them in a letter to the King of Scotland. "There is risen," she said, "a sect of perilous consequences." She was quite right in suspecting the "perilous consequences," for these men were sworn foes of absolutism, unless it was their kind of absolutism. The Puritan had an unalterable propensity first of all to make himself assured that the claims of the Church, modeled on the Word of God, and the demands of pure doctrine were made safe. The State, in the Puritan's mind, was bound to be subordinate to and to minister to the needs and requirements of the Spiritual Covenant, which for him towered above everything else on earth. For that reason the Puritan could not throw himself unconditionally in favor of complete democratic control either in Church or State. The spiritually elect were to be the guardians of both Church and State.

The story of Massachusetts Bay Colony shows how very slowly the dyed-in-the-wool Puritan moved in the direction of granting to the individual the unlimited right to think for himself, or of putting the destiny of the Colony entirely in the hands of the people themselves. A narrow religious franchise excluded four-fifths of the people of Massachusetts Bay Colony from participation in public affairs. The "saints" governed the Colony and felt complete justification in doing it. Herbert A. L. Fisher in his Tercentenary Address in Boston in 1930 put the situation in a crisp sentence: "They spurned democracy, they persecuted conscience, they taxed without consent." [1] How completely they "spurned democracy" can be seen in the measured words of their greatest minister, John Cotton. He wrote: "Democracy I do not conceive that God did ever ordain as fit government either for Church or Commonwealth. If the people be governors who shall be the governed?" G. P. Gooch is thoroughly sound in his judgment when he says

[1] P. 8.

that "Modern Democracy is the child of the Reformation, not of the Reformers." [1] Nevertheless, democracy reaped a great gain from the Puritan movement, though it is not easy to name outstanding individual Puritans who were democratically minded. It is not too much to say that the seeds of democratic institutions were planted deep in the religious life of the colonists of Massachusetts Bay. It was something more than humor when James Russell Lowell said that Puritanism laid the egg from which democracy was hatched. Modern democracy was not achieved by direct aim: it was a slow by-product of the common man's struggle for a Church after his own heart, i. e. a Church in which he himself was a living and creative organ of the Life of God. Democracy as it has taken shape in the world today has its roots deep in the heart of religion.

Many forces and numerous influences coöperated to bring about the revolution which transferred power and authority from the hands of a select few, who were supposed to possess "divine right," to the hands, sometimes unwashed and rough with labor, of the rank and file of common men. The stern necessities that confronted the Huguenots fighting for life, the Presbyterians in Scotland contending for "pure faith," and the Dutch Protestants defending their truth against the powers of Spain compelled all of them to re-

---

[1] *English Democratic Ideas in the Seventeenth Century* (2nd ed.), p. 7.

state their "rights" and their "claims," and out
of the dust and fury of what seemed to them spiritual battles there emerged a clear formulation of
man's rights as man. And when I talk here of
democracy I mean the universal human privilege
to share and enjoy the full rights of citizenship.

This was first most clearly put in Holland, where,
after Dutch liberty had been won from Spain, there
came the best opportunity for a people with reformed faith to work out on a large scale their own
experiment in government. Althusius, like all the
other authorities of the time, was cautious and
often inconsistent, but his formulation of the principles of government first published in 1603 marks
an epoch, and furnished many basic ideas to
Hobbes, Locke, Penn, Algernon Sidney and many
other thinkers in this field. The rights of rule,
Althusius declared, are for the social body neces-
sarily and exclusively its own. Only when it pos-
sesses these rights does a nation live, and when it
loses them it becomes unworthy of the name of
nation. The people, he insisted, are the only think-
able source of majesty and rule. Althusius was the
modern father of the theory of social contract
which was to have a most significant place in human thought during the two hundred years that
followed. I have purposely said that Althusius was
the *modern* father of the social contract theory because this theory had more ancient roots. William
of Occam, a precursor of Wyclif, had already in the
fourteenth century expounded theories of govern-

ment which implicitly held the inalienable and in-
destructible right of popular freedom and sovereignty and a social contract basis.

But it is one thing to formulate noble theories of
life, and quite another to set them into action and
to make the adventure of a practical experiment
with them. Gerrard Winstanley, who was one of
the boldest of the adventurers with these ideas,
finely stated this point in his *Watchword to the City
of London*. "My mind was not at rest," he wrote,
"because nothing was *acted*, and thoughts ran in
me that words and writings are nothing and must
die; for action is the life of all and if thou dost not
act thou dost nothing."

It was in the first instance the plain men of the
yeoman type, trained in the small self-governing
religious groups, who launched the larger experiment of democratic control in England. If the
Parliament party had had its way, and if the attempt of the conservative forces to settle the Pres-
byterian system on the Church had succeeded
throughout the nation, as it did succeed in London
and Lancashire, and the small sects had been suppressed, as they would have been, democratic
principles would almost certainly not have emerged
at this time. It was the fortune of war, the triumph
of the army, that ended the hopes of the conservative Puritan party for uniformity in religion and
for the preservation of a mildly reformed State. It
was just when the Westminster Assembly was
finishing in the Jerusalem Chamber its architec-

tural work of building a Church after the Puritan
model that the portent of a wholly new order of
things became unmistakable. The Westminster
Confession, after the manner of Calvin, inculcated
obedience to "the powers which God hath ordained," but there was a menacing popular sentiment, including almost all of the dissenting sects,
already running counter to such a view. As Gooch
puts it, "the sects that had sprung forth like a harvest of armed men from the soil threw themselves
into opposition to the Presbyterians." [1]

A short tract by Isaac Penington entitled *The
Right, Safety and Liberty of the People*, written in
1651, is a clear and forceful presentation of the
position to which a large number of the sectaries
had by this time arrived. Penington at this date
was a Seeker. His father had been a liberal, a
friend of John Webster and a staunch foe of tyranny, and meantime the son had formed a passion
for popular freedom. "Freedom," he wrote in this
tract, "is of more worth than your estates, yea
than your lives and therefore deserves to be higher
prized. . . . Pursue your Freedom whatever it
costs." In the text of this little known tract the
man who was to become the leading Quaker mystic
of that period announced the basic principles of
Democracy: "They only are a free People who
have their Governments of their own Choyce."
"This right belongs to every People," he asserts,
"though few, if any, are in possession of it." The

---

[1] *English Democratic Ideas*, p. 108.

right of the people, as Penington interprets it, includes three things: the free choice of the government under which they are to live, the establishment of it in successful operation, and the alteration of it as new needs and occasions require. He based his claim to this majestic right on "an inward sense seated in man's nature and guided by the true Light of Reason."

It may be taken for granted that this principle which Penington expounded in 1651 was not an original idea with him. It was the common air which the members of the democratic sects of the era breathed. This tract, with its noble conception of political liberty, stoutly maintains the doctrine so precious to all the sectaries of the time that no civil government, not even Parliament, has any dominion rights in the sphere of religion. These matters belong by inalienable right to the inner tribunal of individual conscience.

The "new model" army which went on from victory to victory, and which held the destiny of the nation in its hands, was composed largely of men of intense religious faith, members of independent self-governing sects and permeated with the spirit of religious freedom. There could obviously be no enforcement of uniformity until the new model army was disbanded. A manifesto drawn up by the army on June 4, 1647, declared that the men who composed it were not mercenaries, hired by arbitrary power, but were "free commoners of England drawn together and continued in arms in judgment and conscience for defense of their own and the peoples' rights and liberties." "We shall not disband nor divide," they further declared, "nor suffer ourselves to be disbanded or divided" until such rights and liberties are secured. That has the significance of a new epoch.

"The State," Cromwell wrote before the battle of Marston Moor, "in choosing men to serve it takes no notice of their opinions." And after the victory of Naseby he wrote to the Speaker of the House of Commons, "Honest men served you faithfully in this action. They are trusty. I beseech you in the name of God not to discourage them. He that ventures his life for the liberty of his country, I wish he [may] trust God for the liberty of his conscience." "All that believe," he wrote later, "have the real unity, which is the most glorious, being inward and spiritual."

With a steadily increasing sense that they had been risking their lives for the principle of religious freedom the soldiers of the new model army pushed on ever farther, increasing in the boldness of their demands for a free and self-governing nation, with the people as "the source of all majesty and rule." "It was the religious struggle," J. R. Green truly says in his *Short History of the English People*, "which drew the political in its train." These men who were standing like adamant for "rights and liberties" cared more intensely for religious rights and privileges than for anything else, but political rights were near kin.

This close connection between the religious ideas of the sectaries and the development of political thought did not escape the attention of the ever watchful Thomas Edwards. He complained in the *Gangraena* that just as these mad people had rejected authority in religion so now they were rejecting it in politics. "As they do in matters of religion and conscience," he says, "fly from the Scriptures and from supernatural truths revealed there, that a man may not be questioned for going against them, but only for errours against the light of nature and right reason; so they do also in civill government and in things of this world, they do fly from the lawes and constitutions of Kingdoms and will be governed by rules according to nature and right reason, and though the lawes and customes of a Kingdome be never so plain and cleer against their wayes, yet will they not submit, but cry out for naturall rights derived from Adam and right reason." [1]

Cromwell's army had become an immense debating society. It was seething with religious and democratic ideas. The main topic of debate was the free man's religion, and the topic which followed close after this first one was man's divine right to settle the form of government for himself and for his nation. The way in which the soldiers drew their conclusions of political freedom from their experience of religious freedom is revealed in a great debate between the representatives of the

[1] *Gangraena*, Part III, p. 20.

common soldiers and the representatives of the army officers, held at Putney at a Grand Council Meeting beginning October 25, 1647. The debate centred about the manifesto which the agitators, both within and outside the army, had drawn up as a new Bill of Rights, called "An Agreement of the People." It contained in germ almost all the democratic-republican principles which were elaborated in later documents and demands. John Lilburne was one of the authors of it. How strongly the religious spirit dominated the debate can be seen by the fact that Lieutenant-Colonel Goffe and Lieutenant-General Cromwell, with the unity of all who were present, called for a solemn day of waiting for the guidance and direction of God in their deliberations. It would appear from the accounts that at least part of the day was spent in deep silent waiting. Cromwell, in a subsequent speech, refers to the custom of "altogether sitting still" when "wee want particular and extraordinary impressions." [1] He proceeds to say, "I thinke that this law (written in the heart) and this word speaking within us — which truly is in every man who hath the spiritt of God — we are to have a regard to." Thomas Bennet of Cambridge University, in his book *An Answer to the Dissenters Pleas for Separation*, says that "Cromwell favored Enthusiasm [by which he means Mysticism] and with six soldiers

---

[1] The Reports of the debate are given in the *Clarke Papers*, edited by C. H. Firth. Printed for the Camden Society (London, 1891). Cromwell's speech referred to above is in Vol. I, pp. 378–383.

preached and prayed at Whitehall . . . and confessed that he prayed according to impulse [i. e. as
he was "moved" by the Spirit], and that not feeling such impulse, which he called supernatural, he
did forbear to pray oftentimes for several days
together." [1] Captain Clarke, another one of the
speakers, after the time of solemn waiting, declared: "Wee should desire noe way, but waite
which way God will lead us." [2]

The leaders of the army came out plumply in the
debate in favor of complete manhood suffrage and
for such a reorganization of the nation that the
people should be put entirely in control of its
destinies. The officers were naturally more conservative than the representatives of the soldiers.
General Ireton stood staunchly for the authority
of those settled engagements which had the sanction of the past, and no less solidly for the established rights of property as against the perils of a
free democracy. Cromwell played the rôle of a
mediator between the radicals and the conservatives, and was all the time bent on finding the will
of God in the matter, turning sometimes to inci-
dents in Scripture and sometimes to what he called
particular impressions. Here is a typical sentence:
"Wee speake as men that desire to have the feare
of God before our eyes, and men that may nott re-
solve to doe that which wee doe in the power of a

[1] I have been able to consult only the fifth edition (London, 1711).
The reference above is to pp. 4–5 of that edition.
[2] *Clarke Papers*, I, 28.

fleshly strength, butt to lay this as the foundation of all our actions, to doe that which is the will of God." [1]

Colonel Rainborow, Mr. Wildman (the conservatives took note of his name), and a Mr. Everard, who was popularly called "Buff-coat," presented the case for a radical change of basis in the direction of complete democracy. Mr. Wildman, who spoke for the army, sounds like a forerunner of Thomas Jefferson. He said: "Wee are now engaged for our freedome; that's the end of Parliaments [i. e. they exist to secure freedom], nott to constitute what is already [established] according to the just rules of government. Every person in England hath as cleere a right to elect his Representative as the greatest person in England. I conceive that's the undeniable maxime of government: *that all government is in the free consent of the people*. If [so] then uppon that account, there is no person that is under a just government, or hath his owne unless hee by his owne free consent bee putt under that Government. This hee cannot bee unlesse hee bee consenting to itt, and therefore according to this maxime there is never a person in England but ought to have a voice in elections; . . . there are noe lawes that in this strictnesse and rigour of justice, any man is bound to that are nott made by those who hee doth consent to. And, therefore, I should humbly move . . . whether any person can justly bee bound by law who doth nott

[1] *Clarke Papers*, I, 248.

give his consent that such persons shall make lawes for him." [1]

Colonel Rainborow, though himself an officer, was the most effective of the army advocates for the complete democratic position. His presentation of the case was vivid and picturesque. Many of the soldiers confessed, as soldiers of all periods have confessed, that in the confusions and crosscurrents of war they did not know what they were fighting for. But Rainborow knew what he had been fighting for, namely that "the poorest hee in England" may enjoy his inalienable rights. "I would faine know," he says, "what wee have fought for," and forthwith he asserts the principle for which he and his companions in arms have exposed themselves to death. "The people of England are enslaved," he asserts, "if they must bee bound by lawes in which they have no voice at all." [2] "I really thinke," he says, "that the poorest hee that is in England hath a life to live as the greatest hee; and therefore truly I thinke it's cleare that every man that is to live under a Government ought first by his owne consent to putt himself under that Government; and I doe thinke that the poorest man in England is nott at all bound in a stricte sence to that Government that hee hath not had a voice to putt himself under. . . . I should doubt whether he was an Englishman or noe who should doubt these thinges." [3] The fathers of our Republic had nothing to say about the rights of the com-

[1] *Clarke Papers*, I, 318.   [2] *Ibid.*, p. 311.   [3] *Ibid.*, p. 301.

mon man that was in advance of the views of this old Ironside soldier.

"Gangraena" Edwards was greatly shocked to find that such views as these of Rainborow were common talk in England. They claim, he declared with horror, that "by naturall birth all men [even the "poorest hee"] are equally and alike born to enjoy propriety [i. e. property], liberty and freedom." Having a birthright by nature from Adam carries with it "the just Rights and Prerogatives of mankind which are propriety, liberty and freedom." [1] Rainborow, however radical he is in his position that "the foundation of all law lies in the people," vigorously protests that he and his companions are not for "anarchy" and do not claim anybody's property, but only stand for the principle "that every man born in England cannot, ought nott, neither by the law of God nor the law of nature, to bee exempted from the choice of those who are to make lawes for him to live under, *and for him, for ought I know, to loose his life under.*" [2]

Cromwell and Ireton, especially Ireton, presented, with much skill and with balance of judgment, the difficulties and dangers involved in the radical democratic position as set forth by Rainborow and his friends. It would not be easy to express better than Ireton did the need to have the safeguards of a property qualification for suffrage, and the chaos that comes when each individual

[1] *Gangraena*, Part III, p. 16.
[2] *Clarke Papers*, I, 305. See also Rainborow's speech, pp. 308–309.

under the guise of liberty follows his own sweet will. One specimen of his elaborate argument will be sufficient to show that the army had good defenders of property rights as well as of the rights of "the poorest hee." "If there be anything att all," Ireton said, "that is a foundation of libertie itt is this, that those who shall chuse the law-makers shall be the men freed from dependence upon others. . . . I thinke if wee from imagination and conceits will go about to hazard the peace of the Kingdom to alter the constitution in such a point, we shall see that libertie that wee soe much talke of and contend for shall bee nothing att all by this our contending for it, *by putting itt into the hands of those that will give it away when they have itt.*" [1]

That point of Ireton's touches very closely the ground of our present disillusionment with democracy. It is eternally difficult to make and to keep democracy "safe," unless the privileges of liberty have cost the individual man something; or to make the voter prize his right of suffrage and use it for noble ends unless he has something at stake in the issue of the election. The sanctions of property seem to Ireton necessary in order to ensure a loyal and intelligent ballot.

Cromwell was concerned on his part to point out the essential difficulty of ever attaining corporate wisdom where capricious individuals are left to follow their own private impulses. This same difficulty attached in Cromwell's mind to the religious

[1] *Clarke Papers*, I, 341.

doctrine of the inward light, and no less urgently
to any form of democracy that puts ultimate power
in the hands of the people, though he was much
more sympathetic with the rights and privileges of
the common man than Ireton was. He significantly declared that he was not "wedded and
glewed" to any fixed particular form of government and that he believed that "Buff-coat" and
the other "agitators" were "aiming at peace and
safetie" and actuated by a good spirit as to their
principles.[1] But, as a practical, straightforward,
common-sense man, he wants to know what assurance there is that the highest interests and welfare
of the nation will be safe on such an unstable
basis. "What do you thinke the consequences
would bee?" he asks. "Would itt nott bee utter
confusion? One county against another?"[2] "Let
every honest man consider," he continues in the
same speech, "whether or noe there be nott very
reall objections in point of difficulty. I know a man
may answer all difficulties with *faith*, and faith will
answer all difficulties where itt is faith, but wee are
very apt all of us to call that faith that may bee
butt carnall imagination and carnall reasonings.
Itt is nott enough to propose thinges that are good
in the end . . . itt is our duty as Christians and
men to consider consequences."

The long and short of the issue is this: What
is the criterion and test that discriminates faith,
divine guidance, and inward light from carnal

---

[1] *Clarke Papers*, I, 277.   [2] *Ibid.*, p. 237.

imagination and selfish desire? Without some stabilizing control would not popular rule end in confusion, one leader pitted against another and the unity of the nation put in jeopardy? So thinks this strong man, himself a ruler of men, but if any one can propose guarantees of stability and wisdom, Cromwell would gladly give every man his fundamental rights and privileges.

Out of this ferment which the army debate reveals, two remarkable tendencies emerged, one in the direction of the discovery of tests and checks and safety devices for stabilizing democracy, and the other in the direction of absolute insistence on *the divine right of man as man*, and on the privilege of "the poorest hee" to have his God-ordained share in the good things of the earth.

I cannot here follow out this first tendency. It is another story. John Milton — another John who was a "beloved disciple" of liberty — was one of the noblest interpreters in the seventeenth century of the doctrine of the sovereignty of the people. His controversial tracts in favor of self-government presented and defended the position that fundamentally political power is the birthright of the people. With breadth of vision and profound insight, nevertheless, he saw clearly that the foundation of a permanent State must have its bases deeper than the temporary impulse of the individual. Through John Locke, Algernon Sidney, William Penn, and the creative statesmen of the English Revolution, the principle of democratic freedom slowly "broadened down from precedent to precedent." The principle of pledges and "engagements" on which Ireton insisted became a recognized principle. The obligations which had accumulated from the inheritance of the past were recognized as binding on the present. The *constitution* of a nation was seen to be an immortal and ever-growing bond, binding past, present, and future into an indissoluble whole of community life. The nation never dies. There must be no erratic, impulsive pursuit of temporary interests, for every generation carries on the obligations of the past and legislates for the welfare of the unborn future. Whether there be a "social contract" or not, life is essentially "conjunct" and there is an undying social obligation. Slowly the checks and restraints of majority responsibility, of a House responsible to the people, of judicial interpretation of constitutional right and justice took shape. Liberty and freedom ceased to be mere capricious and impulsive individual claims. They took their place in a social order, stabilized by law, corporate wisdom, and constitutional obligations. Democracy is still an experiment, but a long line of wise statesmen, working out checks and systems of balance and restraint on capricious freedom, have made it an experiment full of hope and promise.[1]

[1] "Buff-coat", during the army debate, expressed the radical position vigorously in a speech against the tyranny of past "engagements" or obligations. He said that "hee could breake engagements in case they were proved unjust and that itt might appear to his conscience (that they were unjust). That whatsoever hopes or obligations I

"Men, not majorities, make history," has been Mussolini's famous slogan. He means by "men" unique, great men, who by sheer will and genius have dominated their age, have held the masses in awe, or, at least, in subjection. The two extreme religious democrats to whom I shall turn meant just the opposite by the word when they proposed to give all ultimate power and authority to "men" — men for them meant common men, who henceforth were to be proclaimed free and equal. These two remarkable democrats who believed that nations were composed of men were Gerrard Winstanley and John Lilburne — still another John, but this time not always "beloved," though he certainly was an honest "disciple of liberty."

Winstanley was born at Wigan in Lancashire in 1609. He was not a University man, but he possessed remarkable original capacity and power and developed a beautiful quality of spirit; when at his best he shows a quite extraordinary style of literary expression. He had periods of profound psychic experience of a mystical type, when specific messages and auditions seemed to break in on his consciousness and to give him a palpable sense that he was called to be a "prophet." He declares that he was filled with "abundance of quiet peace and secret joy." But his mystical openings did not carry him up into an ecstatic union with God.

should bee bound unto, if afterwards God should reveale Himself I would breake itt speedily, if itt were 100 a day." *Clarke Papers*, I, 273.

They rather pushed him out into a spirit of suffering love with his fellow-men. Like John Woolman, he formed a central aspiration to "turn all he possessed [including himself] into the channel of universal love." He is quite saturated with the phrases and ideas and many of the practices that took form a little later in the Quaker movement. He calls his little group of followers "Children of the Light," and proclaims Christ as the Light and Life in every man. He insisted, like any good seventeenth-century Quaker, in wearing his hat in the presence of magistrates and army officers. "The Spirit of Reason," he wrote in *The Saint's Paradise*, "is not without [i. e. outside] a man, but within every man; hence he need not run after others to tell him or teach him; for this Spirit is his maker and dwells in him." In his unillumined days he looked for God as a Being "beyond the sun and stars," "a God outside," but in his later period he has come to see and know Him as a Spirit "ruling within" and "dwelling in every man and woman." "You believe in Christ," he said, "when the actings and breathings of your soul are within the centre of the same Spirit in which the man Jesus Christ lived, acted and breathed." "You will never have rest in your soul," he wrote, in the *New Law of Righteousness*, "until God speaks *in you*."

It is, however, not Winstanley the mystic and saint that concerns us now; it is Winstanley the democrat and "digger." He was the author and finisher of a new Utopia which was aimed to strike at the very root of monarchy and aristocracy and inaugurate a genuine reign of the people. He was an uncompromising communist, but it was to be a communism based on love and good will and set up and maintained by gentle forces of sympathetic sharing and coöperating. In his *Letter to General Fairfax and his Council of War* Winstanley said: "I hate none, I love all, I delight to see every one live comfortably, I would have none live in poverty, straits or sorrows. Therefore, if you find any selfishness in this work, or anything that is destructive to the whole creation, I would that you would open your hearts as freely to me as I have been open-hearted in declaring that which I find much life and strength in. But if you see Righteousness in it, then own it and let the power of Love have his freedom and glory."

His utopian masterpiece is *The Law of Freedom in a Platform*, with a "Dedicatory Epistle." to Oliver Cromwell. "The Spirit of the whole creation," which is God, he declares, "is about the reformation of the World, and He will go forward with His work." He proceeds to point out that two alternatives confront Cromwell: "Either set the land free to the oppressed commoners who assisted you and paid the army their wages . . . or secondly you must only remove the conqueror's power out of the king's hand into other men's, maintaining the old laws still. And then [if this second course is followed] your wisdom and honor are blasted forever and you will either lose yourself or lay the foundation of greater slavery to posterity. . . . Either you must establish Commonwealth's freedom in power, making provision for every one's peace which is righteousness, or else you must set up monarchy again."

He held that there are certain "unalienable creation-rights" which belong to every human being and one of these birth-principles, Winstanley maintained, was the right to dig, plow, and plant the common, unused public land of England, so that "every man may have nourishment and preservation in the free use of the earth."

As I have stated earlier, Winstanley was not satisfied to spin out utopian theories in words and in books. He boldly struck out and put his ideas into action. With a little band of followers in 1649 he and William Everard started to dig up and plant the common land on George Hill in Surrey, for which they were arrested and fined nearly ten pounds. Winstanley and two of his friends addressed an appeal to the House of Commons, asking "whether the common people shall have the quiet enjoyment of the Commons, or Waste land, or whether they shall be under the will of Lords of the Manor still." Meantime, under Winstanley's contagious call to action, "digging" broke out in Buckinghamshire, Middlesex, Hertfordshire, and Berkshire, altogether in thirty-four towns. One of the most interesting documents of the "Diggers" is a Declaration signed by nine men who are "Poor Inhabitants" in the town of Wellingborow in

Northamptonshire. They say: "Now we consider that the Earth is our mother and that God hath given it to the children of men and that the common and waste grounds belong to the poor and that we have a right to the common ground both from the Law of the Land, Reason and Scriptures; therefore we have begun to bestow our righteous labor upon it . . . resolving not to dig up any man's property until they freely give us it. . . . Our desire is that some that approve of this work of righteousness would but spread this our declaration before the great Council of the Land. That they may be pleased to give us more encouragement."

Winstanley's scheme included free education for all the children in common schools, with special vocational training for all who intended to take up trades or to work in industries. He proposed to remove all ecclesiastical control and to set religion completely free. He dreamed of eliminating rivalry and competition in business and of producing a new society in which there would be meat and drink and clothes and dwellings for all who were born into the world. In his gentleness and tenderness he would banish poverty from the earth. Wars were to cease and there should be henceforth peace among all men of good will.

Lilburne was a very different type of man. Meekness and gentleness were not his by nature. Carlyle called him "a stirring man; very flamy and very fulginous." One would hardly say of him that he did "not strive or cry or lift up his voice in the street." Hume's line about him puts the truth as well as one could put it: "He was the most turbulent, but most upright and courageous of human kind." He was twice tried for high treason, but acquitted each time by juries whose rights and authority he boldly vindicated before the Court. He was not a mystic like Winstanley nor a saint like John Everard, but he was profoundly religious, deriving his political democracy primarily from his experience of self-government in the religious sects. He became a Quaker toward the end of his life, and was a friend of gentle Richard Hubberthorne. His funeral was held in the "Bull and Mouth" Meeting House in 1657, and four thousand Friends accompanied the body to its grave in the new Quaker burying ground.

He was born in the County of Durham in 1618. He had a stormy youth: was whipped, pilloried, fined, and loaded with irons by order of the Star Chamber for his connection with the printing of the *Merry Liturgy*. He had a distinguished career as a soldier in the first Civil War and became lieutenant-colonel. At this time he was a friend and admirer of Cromwell. He soon became disillusioned over the results of the war and was convinced that the struggle, so costly in lives and treasure, was leading to no adequate goal. Whereupon he came forward as the foremost defender of the claims of the soldiers and of the common people who were with the army in aim and spirit.

It was to Lilburne's propaganda, more than to any
other influence, that the army awoke to its consciousness of unattained rights and the claims
which were expressed in "The Agreement of the
People" and the Putney Debate of 1647.

Lilburne's enemies coined the nickname "Levellers" to discredit the popular party which he championed. There were, no doubt, wild elements in this
movement for popular liberties, and the agitators
pushed on toward extremes that were dangerous
in a society that was unprepared and untrained
for the full exercise of freedom. But Lilburne
and his followers vigorously disclaimed any intention of bringing all men and all property to a
uniform level. They asserted that the term Levellers applied to them was unfair and unjust. They
said, "Equal justice, impartially distributed to all
men, this is the levelling aimed at," and present-
day historians are coming to agree that Lilburne
was an honest and uncorrupted, though perhaps
over-strenuous, champion of justice for the common people. He subscribed himself "an honest and
true-bred, free Englishman, that never in his life
feared a tyrant, nor loved an oppressor," [1] and that
confession states the actual fact. In the *Second
Part of Englands New-Chaines Discovered*, the
author states in a dignified way that the word
"leveller" was framed and cast upon all persons
who were opposed to tyranny. The inventors of

[1] *The Legal Fundamental Liberties of the People of England, Revived, Asserted and Vindicated by John Lilburne*, June 8, 1649, p. 75.

the term, he says, have industriously propagated false ideas and have insinuated many slanders about them into credulous hearts. It was almost certainly due to this "great Commoner" and his party that democratic principles were pushed into the foreground of the Commonwealth struggle and that the rights of the people received such definite formulation at this early stage. Lilburne's dominating vision was the establishment in England of a democratic government, limited and bounded by law, with a written constitution, originating in a compact of the sovereign people, and, finally, interpreted by an independent and impartial judicial court. His idea of a written Constitution grew out of the "Covenants" of the free Congregational churches, and he proposed to transfer to the sphere of politics all the principles that had been tried out and tested in the sphere of religion.

His plan, like that of Winstanley, involved a scheme of complete popular education, for he saw that the strength of tyranny lay in popular ignorance. Lilburne was the first person to attempt to carry out in practical politics the doctrinaire theory of social contract. His central idea throughout his stormy career was the people's control of government by a paramount law originating in themselves,[1] so that he and his Levellers, or Rationalists, as they called themselves, deserve an important place in the history of constitutional thought. Lilburne was the sworn foe of tithes and

[1] T. C. Pease, *The Leveller Movement*, p. 215.

of all parliamentary control of religion. He advocated the abolition of imprisonment for debt, and abolition of capital punishment for every crime except murder. He took the ground that the penalties of the law should be definite, that no one should be compelled to testify against himself, that all prisoners should have counsel, and that the people themselves should have a voice in the declaration of war. By pen and by actual practice, he expounded and defended the rights of juries to make their own untrammeled decision. He pushed to the limit the sovereignty of the people and their fundamental right to a deliberate share in all matters of life, welfare, and security.

More than any other man of the period Lilburne was the leader of the people's party, the champion of their hopes, and their hero. The immense popular outburst on the occasion of Lilburne's imprisonment in Newgate in 1645 was a great surprise to all who were in authority, for it revealed the fact that liberal and radical ideas were not confined to the army. The people rose up and issued a manifesto, with the following title: *Remonstrance of many thousand of citizens and other freeborn people to their own House of Commons, occasioned through the illegal imprisonment of that famous and worthy sufferer for his country's freedom, John Lilburne . . . calling their Commissioners in Parliament to account how they [since the beginning of their session to this present] have discharged their duties to the Universality of the People, their sovereign Lord, from whom their power and strength is derived and by whose favour it is continued* (London, July 7, 1646). The spirit of the men who wrote and signed that document sounds very much like what we in America call "the spirit of '76"!

The Presbyterians in Parliament, feeling the pulse of public sentiment and wishing to make use of Lilburne's hostility to Cromwell, succeeded in having Parliament vote a large compensation in the form of confiscated lands to Lilburne soon after his release from imprisonment. But "honest John" was not a man who could be bought or corrupted. He was absolutely dedicated to a principle and nothing could swerve him from the idol of his heart. Almost immediately after his release from prison he wrote to Cromwell: "Although, if I prosecuted or desired revenge for an hard and almost starving imprisonment, I could have had of late the choice of twenty opportunities to have paid you to the purpose, I scorn it, especially when you are low, and this assure yourself, that if ever my hand be upon you, it shall be when you are in your full glory, if then you shall decline from the righteous way of Truth and Justice, which, if you will fixedly and impartially prosecute, I am yours, to the last drop of my heart's blood (for all your late severe hand toward me). John Lilburne."

After the publication of the *Second Part of Englands New Chaines-Discovered*, Lilburne and three of his associates were arrested and committed to the Tower. Lilburne's trial for sedition in October,

1649, was one of the famous trials in history. The prisoner stood up in Court as a free man and interpreted the fundamental rights of an Englishman and the scope and status of a jury. When the jury announced his acquittal the people raised a shout of joy which lasted a half hour and which made the judges turn pale. The acclaim of the people followed him all the way from the Guild Hall to the Tower. A commemorative medal, bearing the inscription: "John Lilburne saved by the Lord and the integrity of his Jury," was struck off in his honor by the joyous populace. His final trial in 1652 brought forth even greater popular support, and gave Lilburne a fresh opportunity to expand his theory of the rights of juries. An even more significant feature of this trial was Lilburne's pertinacious insistence that he should have the opportunity to see and study his writ of indictment before the trial, a point on which he won. Once more his acquittal called forth extraordinary rejoicing on the part of the people, while Cromwell is said to have regarded it as a greater defeat than the loss of a battle.[1] By this time the old fighter for the liberties of the people had become a Quaker and had renounced all weapons except the sword of the Spirit.

In the meantime the American colonies were the laboratories in which these dangerous doctrines of democracy were being tried out in a succession of

[1] Technically Lilburne was "acquitted but not set free." It was death that set him free.

practical experiments. It was on this side of the ocean that the self-governing Church grew by a kind of process of nature into the self-governing State. On the *Mayflower* the Pilgrim Fathers, still under the spell of John Robinson's great words about the breaking forth of more light, by a solemn covenant formed themselves into a civil body politic, and launched, not "a new Jerusalem," but a new England in which "the poorest hee" was to have his voice in shaping the destiny of the colonial commonwealth. The servants and common sailors on the ship signed the covenant with the noblest of the party, and gave their votes for the first governor and council.

Roger Williams, after he had weathered his great tribulations, set about the task of building a free and autonomous city-state. "For our common peace and welfare," the inhabitants of the little colony declared, "we will subject ourselves in active or passive obedience to such orders and agreements as shall be made by the greater number of the present householders, and such as shall be hereafter admitted by their consent into the same privilege and covenant in our ordinary meeting." The decisions, however, of this body politic were forever to be confined to "civil things," since a man's conscience was to be free and his relation with his God was to be in his own hands. Roger Williams' first charter gave the people "power to rule themselves as they should find most suitable to themselves"

— "a government held by the free consent of all, or the greater part of the free inhabitants."

"The Fundamental Orders of Connecticut," drawn up by Hooker, also provided for a commonwealth built on the same basis as the free Congregational Church. The Massachusetts Bay Colony, at first strongly theocratic, moved steadily forward toward democracy. The narrow, exclusive franchise was abolished in 1691. The harder lines maintained by the dominant clergy yielded gradually to the growing enlightenment of the common citizen, who, however humble, had the privileges of education at Harvard. Everybody freely discussed every issue of Church and Commonwealth, while the town meeting became a training place for democracy and statesmanship. Nine years before the extension of suffrage in Massachusetts, William Penn had begun his "holy experiment" in Pennsylvania, with the power of government "put entirely in the hands of the people." In a famous letter to a friend, Penn had declared: "For the matters of liberty and privilege I purpose that which is extraordinary and [to] leave myself and succession no power of doing mischief, that the will of one man may not hinder the good of a whole country."

The other colonies were not far behind in faith or vision. And when the constitutional Republic startled Europe with its bold experiment in popular government toward the close of the eighteenth century there had already been more than a century and a half of intensive preparation for the immense adventure. The college, the schoolhouse, the town meeting, the Assembly, the debating society, and the free discussion in the country grocery store had given the common man enviable wisdom for the business of citizenship. Not the least factor in his maturing preparation for public responsibility had been his training in the management and direction of his autonomous, democratic Church.

INDEX

INDEX

INDEX